R Graphs Cookbook

Detailed hands-on recipes for creating the most useful types of graphs in R—starting from the simplest versions to more advanced applications

Hrishi V. Mittal

[PACKT] PUBLISHING

open source*
community experience distilled

BIRMINGHAM - MUMBAI

R Graphs Cookbook

First published: January 2011

Production Reference: 1110111

Published by Packt Publishing Ltd.
32 Lincoln Road
Olton
Birmingham, B27 6PA, UK.

ISBN 978-1-849513-06-7

www.packtpub.com

Cover Image by Charwak (charwak86@gmail.com)

Credits

Author
Hrishi V. Mittal

Reviewers
Patrick Burns
Paul Butler
Markus Loecher
Paolo Sonego

Acquisition Editor
Eleanor Duffy

Development Editor
Maitreya Bhakal

Technical Editor
Vanjeet D'souza

Copy Editor
Neha Shetty

Editorial Team Leader
Akshara Aware

Project Team Leader
Priya Mukherji

Project Coordinator
Jovita Pinto

Proofreader
Joanna McMahon

Indexer
Tejal Daruwale

Production Coordinator
Melwyn D'sa
Aparna Bhagat

Cover Work
Melwyn D'sa

About the Author

Hrishi V. Mittal has been working with R for a few years in different capacities. He was introduced to the exciting world of data analysis with R when he was working as a Senior Air Quality Scientist at King's College London, where he used R extensively to analyze large amounts of air pollution and traffic data to inform the Mayor of London's Air Quality Strategy. He has experience in various other programming languages, but prefers R for data analysis and visualization. He is actively involved in various R mailing lists, forums and the development of some R packages.

In early 2010, Hrishi started Pretty Graph Limited (`www.prettygraph.com`), a software company specializing in web-based data visualization products. The company's flagship product, Pretty Graph, uses R as the backend engine for helping researchers and businesses visualize and analyze data. The goal is to bring the power of R to a wider audience by providing a modern graphical user interface which can be accessed by anyone and from anywhere simply by using a web browser.

First and foremost, I am grateful to the creators of R, Ross Ihaka and Robert Gentleman, and the countless other contributors who have made one of the greatest open source software of all time.

I would like to thank my wife Louise for her patience and support throughout the writing of the book. Her feedback on the writing itself has also been very useful. Special thanks are also due to Clive and Jimmy, who have consistently provided silent, warm and furry stress relief.

I'm grateful to my parents and sister for their love and the pride they always take in my work, even when they are not quite sure what I'm doing.

It's been nice to have support from my friends Madhavi Bhargava, Rohit Menon and Aniruddha Kembavi, who have been very encouraging and at times more excited than me about the book.

I'd also like to thank the reviewers for pointing out some errors and suggesting valuable improvements. Last, but not least, I'd like to thank my editor Eleanor Duffy and the rest of the team at Packt, who have been very professional, understanding and helpful throughout the project.

About the Reviewers

Patrick Burns is well known in the R community, in particular for the free R documents that are available on the Burns Statistics website (`http://www.burns-stat.com/`). He produces software for the fund management industry that runs in R and S+.

Paul Butler studies math and computer science at the University of Waterloo in Canada. Between academic terms, he has worked on data analysis and data infrastructure projects at a handful of startups and a large dot-com company. Paul enjoys sailing and bouldering, and blogs sporadically at `http://paulbutler.org/`

Markus Loecher is an expert in predictive modeling and statistical analysis of primarily spatiotemporal data. He holds multiple patents in machine learning and has over nine years of experience analyzing large, complex data sets to build advanced descriptive and predictive models.

Markus holds a BSc from the University of Cologne, a PhD in Physics from Ohio University and a Masters in Statistics from Rutgers University. He completed postdoctoral research in physics at Ohio State University and at Georgia Tech investigating spatiotemporal chaos. His work has been published in several prestigious journals, he has authored on the topic of noise sustained patterns, and co-authored a book on chaos control.

Markus holds R in the highest regard and has been using it actively for about eight years. He is the author of several popular R packages, such as `RgoogleMaps`, `HTMLUtils` and `gbmParallel`. He is the author of *Noise Sustained Patterns* published by World Scientific.

Paolo Sonego has spent the last three years as a bioinformatician analyzing '-omics' data for a company in Trieste, Italy. He is a strong supporter and enthusiast of the R programming language for statistical computing and graphics. He has a blog devoted to his favorite programming language (`onertipaday.blogspot.com`). Paolo lives with his love Flavia and his cat Tristan in Pordenone, Italy.

I want to thank Ross Ihaka and Robert Gentleman for creating R and the wonderful community of both developers and contributors!

www.PacktPub.com

Support files, eBooks, discount offers, and more

You might want to visit www.PacktPub.com for support files and downloads related to your book.

Did you know that Packt offers eBook versions of every book published, with PDF and ePub files available? You can upgrade to the eBook version at www.PacktPub.com and as a print book customer, you are entitled to a discount on the eBook copy. Get in touch with us at service@packtpub.com for more details.

At www.PacktPub.com, you can also read a collection of free technical articles, sign up for a range of free newsletters, and receive exclusive discounts and offers on Packt books and eBooks.

http://PacktLib.PacktPub.com

Do you need instant solutions to your IT questions? PacktLib is Packt's online digital book library. Here, you can access, read and search across Packt's entire library of books.

Why Subscribe?

- Fully searchable across every book published by Packt
- Copy & paste, print and bookmark content
- On demand and accessible via web browser

Free Access for Packt account holders

If you have an account with Packt at www.PacktPub.com, you can use this to access PacktLib today and view nine entirely free books. Simply use your login credentials for immediate access.

Table of Contents

Table of Contents

Preface

With more than two million users worldwide, R is one of *the* most popular open source projects. It is a free and robust statistical programming environment with very powerful graphical capabilities. Analyzing and visualizing data with R is a necessary skill for anyone doing any kind of statistical analysis, and this book will help you do just that in the easiest and most efficient way possible.

Unlike other books on R, this book takes a practical hands-on approach and will dive straight into creating graphs in R right from the very first page. If you wish to harness the power of this mighty open source programming language to visually present and analyze your data in the best way possible—this book is going to show you how.

The *R Graphs Cookbook* takes a practical approach to teaching how to create effective and useful graphs using R. It will demystify a lot of difficult and confusing R functions and parameters. It will enable you to construct and modify data graphics to suit your analysis, presentation, and publication needs.

This practical guide begins by teaching you how to make basic graphs in R and progresses through subsequent dedicated chapters about each graph type in depth. You will learn all about making graphics such as scatter plots, line graphs, bar charts, pie charts, dot plots, heat maps, histograms, and box plots. In addition, there are detailed recipes on making various combinations and advanced versions of these graphs. Dedicated chapters on polishing and finalizing graphs will enable you to produce professional quality graphs for presentation and publication. With the *R Graphs Cookbook* in hand, making graphs in R has never been easier.

What this book covers

Chapter 1, Basic Graph Functions introduces recipes for some basic types of graphs, useful in almost any kind of data analysis. We will go through all the steps to get you going from reading your data into R, making a first graph, tweaking it to suit your needs, and then saving and exporting it for use in presentations and publications.

Chapter 2, Beyond the Basics: Adjusting Key Parameters looks more closely at various arguments to graph functions and their values, highlighting common pitfalls and workarounds. The par () function is explained with some useful examples showing how to adjust colors, sizes, margins, and styles of various graph elements such as points, lines, bars, axes, and titles.

The subsequent chapters 3 to 9 cover the graph types introduced in the first two chapters in more detail.

Chapter 3, Creating Scatter Plots has over a dozen recipes covering scatter plots, which are some of the simplest and most commonly used type of graphs in data analysis. We will see how we can make more enhanced plots by adjusting various arguments and using some new functions.

Chapter 4, Creating Line Graphs and Time Series Charts discusses some more intermediate to advanced recipes for customizing line graphs, improving and speeding up line graphs with multiple lines, processing dates to make time series charts, sparklines and stock charts.

Chapter 5, Creating Bar, Dot, and Pie Charts will show you how you can create many useful variations of bar graphs and dot plots by using only the base library functions. We will also look at a few recipes addressing common criticisms of pie charts with some ways to make them more readable.

Chapter 6, Creating Histograms enhances the basic histogram in R by changing the plotting mode and bins, in addition to style adjustments. We will also look at some advanced recipes combining histograms with other types of graphs.

Chapter 7, Creating Box and Whisker Plots looks into various stylistic and structural adjustments to box plots. We will start by looking at some basic arguments to change individual aspects of a box plot and slowly move to more advanced recipes involving the use of multiple function calls.

Chapter 8, Creating Heat Maps and Contour Plots discusses various types of heat maps for visualizing correlations, trends and multivariate data, and contour plots for showing topographical information in various two-dimensional and three-dimensional ways.

Chapter 9, Creating Maps builds on top of the introduction to visualizing data on geographical maps in the first chapter, covering recipes for plotting data from the World Bank, World Health Organization (WHO), Google Maps API, and some Geographical Information Systems (GIS).

Chapter 10, Finalizing Graphs for Publications and Presentations discusses some tricks and tips to add some polish to our graphs so that they can be used for publication and presentation. We will cover many important practical topics such as exported graph file formats, high resolution formats, vector formats such as PDF, SVG, and PS, mathematical and scientific notations, text descriptions, fonts, graph templates, and themes.

What you need for this book

The only software needed for this book is R itself, which is available for download for all major operating systems at `http://cran.r-project.org`. Some additional R packages are required, but these can be installed from within R. The instructions are provided in the relevant sections of the book.

You will also need the example datasets, which can be downloaded from the book's companion website: `https://www.packtpub.com/r-graph-cookbook/book`.

Who this book is for

This book is for readers already familiar with the basics of R and want to learn the best techniques and code to create graphics in R in the best way possible. It will also serve as an invaluable reference book for expert R users.

Conventions

In this book, you will find a number of styles of text that distinguish between different kinds of information. Here are some examples of these styles, and an explanation of their meaning.

Code words in text are shown as follows: " We will use the base graphics function `hist()` to make our histogram."

A block of code is set as follows:

```
hist(air$Nitrogen.Oxides,
breaks=20,
xlab="Nitrogen Oxide Concentrations",
main="Distribution of Nitrogen Oxide Concentrations")
```

When we wish to draw your attention to a particular part of a code block, the relevant lines or items are set in bold:

```
hist(air$Nitrogen.Oxides,
breaks=20,
xlab="Nitrogen Oxide Concentrations",
main="Distribution of Nitrogen Oxide Concentrations")
```

New terms and important words are shown in bold. Words that you see on the screen, in menus or dialog boxes for example, appear in the text like this: "Select an appropriate mirror site from the **CRAN mirror** window."

Warnings or important notes appear in a box like this.

Tips and tricks appear like this.

Reader feedback

Feedback from our readers is always welcome. Let us know what you think about this book—what you liked or may have disliked. Reader feedback is important for us to develop titles that you really get the most out of.

To send us general feedback, simply send an e-mail to feedback@packtpub.com, and mention the book title via the subject of your message.

If there is a book that you need and would like to see us publish, please send us a note in the SUGGEST A TITLE form on www.packtpub.com or e-mail suggest@packtpub.com.

If there is a topic that you have expertise in and you are interested in either writing or contributing to a book, see our author guide on www.packtpub.com/authors.

Customer support

Now that you are the proud owner of a Packt book, we have a number of things to help you to get the most from your purchase.

Downloading the example code for this book

You can download the example code files for all Packt books you have purchased from your account at http://www.PacktPub.com. If you purchased this book elsewhere, you can visit http://www.PacktPub.com/support and register to have the files e-mailed directly to you.

Errata

Although we have taken every care to ensure the accuracy of our content, mistakes do happen. If you find a mistake in one of our books—maybe a mistake in the text or the code—we would be grateful if you would report this to us. By doing so, you can save other readers from frustration and help us improve subsequent versions of this book. If you find any errata, please report them by visiting http://www.packtpub.com/support, selecting your book, clicking on the errata submission form link, and entering the details of your errata. Once your errata are verified, your submission will be accepted and the errata will be uploaded on our website, or added to any list of existing errata, under the Errata section of that title. Any existing errata can be viewed by selecting your title from http://www.packtpub.com/support.

Piracy

Piracy of copyright material on the Internet is an ongoing problem across all media. At Packt, we take the protection of our copyright and licenses very seriously. If you come across any illegal copies of our works, in any form, on the Internet, please provide us with the location address or website name immediately so that we can pursue a remedy.

Please contact us at copyright@packtpub.com with a link to the suspected pirated material.

We appreciate your help in protecting our authors, and our ability to bring you valuable content.

Questions

You can contact us at questions@packtpub.com if you are having a problem with any aspect of the book, and we will do our best to address it.

1
Basic Graph Functions

In this chapter, we will cover the following recipes:

- ▸ Creating scatter plots
- ▸ Creating line graphs
- ▸ Creating bar charts
- ▸ Creating histograms and density plots
- ▸ Creating box plots
- ▸ Adjusting X and Y axis limits
- ▸ Creating heat maps
- ▸ Creating pairs plots
- ▸ Creating multiple plot matrix layouts
- ▸ Adding and formatting legends
- ▸ Creating graphs with maps
- ▸ Saving and exporting graphs

Introduction

In this chapter, we will see how to use R to make some very basic types of graphs, which are likely to be used in almost any kind of analysis. The recipes in this chapter will give you a feel for how much can be accomplished with very little R code, which is one big reason why R is a good choice for an analysis platform.

Although the examples in this chapter are of a basic nature, we will go through all the steps to get you going from reading your data into R, making a first graph, tweaking it to suit your needs, and then saving and exporting it for use in presentations and publications.

First and foremost, you need to download and install R on your computer. All R packages are hosted on the **Comprehensive R Archive Network** or **CRAN** (http://cran.r-project.org/). R is available for all the three major operating systems at the following locations on the web:

- ▶ Windows: http://cran.r-project.org/bin/windows/base/
- ▶ Linux: http://cran.r-project.org/bin/linux/
- ▶ Mac OS X: http://cran.r-project.org/bin/macosx/

Please read the FAQs (http://cran.r-project.org/faqs.html) and manuals (http://cran.r-project.org/manuals.html) on the CRAN site for detailed help on installation.

Just having the base installation of R should set you up for all the recipes in this book.

Please note that the R code in this book has some comments explaining the code. Any text on a line following the # symbol is treated by R as a comment. For example, you may see something like this:

```
col="yellow" #Setting the color to yellow
```

As you can see clearly, the text after the # explains what the code is doing. Setting the color to yellow in this case. Comments are a way of documenting code so that others reading your code can understand it better. It also serves to help you and you can also understand your code better when you come back to it after a long period of time. Please read each line of code carefully and look out for any comments that will help you understand the code better.

Creating scatter plots

This recipe describes how to make scatter plots using some very simple commands. We'll go from a single line of code, which makes a scatter plot from pre-loaded data, to a script of a few lines that produces a scatter plot customized with colors, titles, and axes limits specified by us.

Getting ready

All you need to do to get started is start R. You should have the R prompt on your screen as shown in the following screenshot:

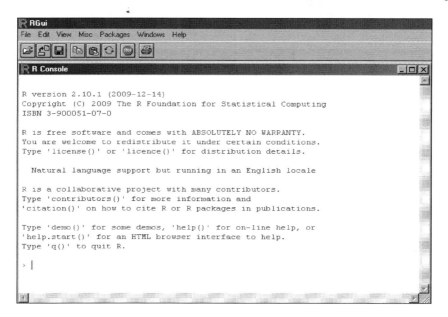

How to do it...

Let's use one of R's inbuilt datasets called `cars` to look at the relationship between the speed of cars and the distances taken to stop (recorded in the 1920s).

To make your first scatter plot, type the following command at the R prompt:

```
plot(cars$dist~cars$speed)
```

This should bring up a window with the following graph showing the relationship between the distance travelled by cars plotted with their speeds:

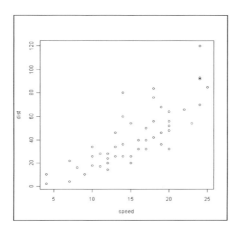

Now, let's tweak the graph to make it look better. Type the following code at the R prompt:

```
plot(cars$dist~cars$speed, # y~x
main="Relationship between car distance & speed", # Plot Title
xlab="Speed (miles per hour)", #X axis title
ylab="Distance travelled (miles)", #Y axis title
xlim=c(0,30), #Set x axis limits from 0 to 30
ylim=c(0,140), #Set y axis limits from 0 to 140
xaxs="i", #Set x axis style as internal
yaxs="i", #Set y axis style as internal
col="red", #Set the color of plotting symbol to red
pch=19) #Set the plotting symbol to filled dots
```

This should produce the following result:

How it works...

R comes preloaded with many datasets. In the example, we used one such dataset called `cars`, which has two columns of data, with the names `speed` and `dist`. To see the data, simply type cars at the R prompt and press *Enter*:

```
>cars
    speed  dist
1       4     2
2       4    10
3       7     4
4       7    22
.  .  .
47     24    92
```

```
48      24      93
49      24      120
50      25      85
>
```

As the output from the R command line shows, the `cars` dataset has two columns and 50 rows of data.

The `plot()` command is the simplest way to make scatter plots (and other types of plots as we'll see in a moment).

In the first example, we simply pass the `x` and `y` arguments that we want to plot in the form `plot(y~x)` that is, we want to plot distance versus speed. This produces a simple scatter plot. In the second example, we pass a few additional arguments that provide R with more information on how we want the graph to look.

The `main` argument sets the plot title, `xlab` and `ylab` set the X and Y axes titles respectively, `xlim` and `ylim` set the minimum and maximum values of the labels on the X and Y axes respectively, `xaxs` and `yaxs` set the style of the axes, `col` and `pch` set the scatter plot symbol color and type respectively. All of these arguments and more will be explained in detail in *Chapter 2, Beyond the Basics*.

There's more...

Instead of the `plot(y~x)` notation used in the preceding examples, you can also use `plot(x,y)`. For more details on all the arguments the `plot()` command can take, see the help documentation by typing `?plot` or `help(plct)` at the R prompt, after plotting the first dataset with `plot()`.

If you want to plot another set of points on the same graph, say from another dataset or the same data points but with another symbol on top, you can use the `points()` function:

```
points(cars$dist~cars$speed,pch=3)
```

A note on R's inbuilt datasets

In addition to the cars dataset used in the example, R has many more datasets, which come as part of the base installation in a package called datasets. To see the complete list of available datasets, call the `data()` function simply by running it at the R prompt:

```
data()
```

See also

Scatter plots are covered in a lot more detail in *Chapter 3, Creating Scatter Plots*.

Creating line graphs

Line graphs are generally used for looking at trends in data over time, so the X variable is usually time expressed as time of the day, date, month, year, and so on. In this recipe, we will see how we can quickly plot such data using the same `plot()` function, which was used in the previous recipe to make scatter plots.

Getting ready

First we need to load the `dailysales.csv` example data file. You can download this file from the code download section of the book's companion website:

```
sales<-read.csv("dailysales.csv", header=TRUE)
```

As the file name suggests, it contains daily sales data of a product. It has two columns: a date column and a sales column showing the number of units sold.

How to do it...

Here's the code to make your first line graph:

```
plot(sales$units~as.Date(sales$date,"%d/%m/%y"),
type="l", #Specify type of plot as l for line
main="Unit Sales in the month of January 2010",
xlab="Date",
ylab="Number of units sold",
col="blue")
```

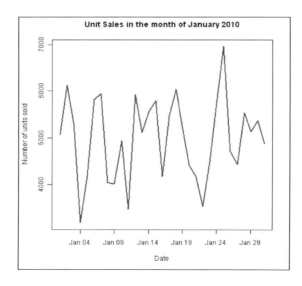

How it works...

We first read the data file using the `read.csv()` function. We passed two arguments to the function: the name of the file we want to read (`dailysales.csv` in double quotes) and with `header=TRUE` we specified that the first row contains column headings. We read the contents of the file and saved it in an object called `sales` with the left arrow notation.

You must have noticed that the plotting code is quite similar to that for producing a scatter plot. The main difference is that this time we passed the `type` argument. The `type` argument tells the `plot()` function whether you want to plot points, lines, or other symbols. It can take nine different values.

 Please see the help section on `plot()` for more details. The default value of type is `"p"` as in points.

If the type is not specified R assumes you want to plot points as it did in the scatter plot example.

The most important part of the example is the way we read the date using the `as.Date()` function. Reading dates in R is a bit tricky. R doesn't automatically recognize date formats. The `as.Date()` function takes two arguments: the first is the variable which contains the date values and the second is the format the date values are stored in. In the example, the dates are in the form date/month/year or dd/mm/yyyy, which we specified as `%d/%m/%y` in the function call. If the date was in mm/dd/yyyy format, we'd use `%m/%d/%y`.

The plot and axes titles and line color are set using the same arguments as for the scatter plot.

There's more...

If you want to plot another line on the same graph, say daily sales data of a second product, you can use the `lines()` function:

```
lines(sales$units2~as.Date(sales$date,"%d/%m/%y"),
col`="red")
```

See also

Line graphs and time series charts are covered in depth in *Chapter 4, Creating Line Graphs and Time Series Plots*.

Creating bar charts

In this recipe, we will learn how to make bar plots, which are useful for visualizing summary data across various categories, such as sales of products or results of elections.

Getting ready

First we need to load the `citysales.csv` example data file. You can download this file from the code download section of the book's companion website:

```
sales<-read.csv("citysales.csv",header=TRUE)
```

How to do it...

Just like the `plot()` function we used to make scatter plots and line graphs in the earlier recipes, the `barplot()` and `dotchart()` functions are part of the base graphics library in R. This means that we don't need to install any additional packages or libraries to use these functions.

We can make bar plots using the `barplot()` function as follows:

```
barplot(sales$ProductA,
names.arg= sales$City,
col="black")
```

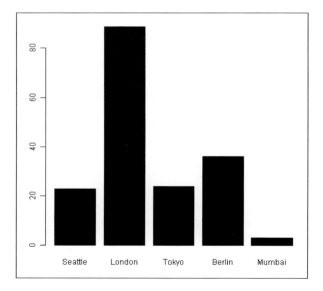

The default setting of orientation for bars is vertical. To change the bars to horizontal, use the `horiz` argument (by default, it is set to `FALSE`):

```
barplot(sales$ProductA,
names.arg= sales$City,
horiz=TRUE,
col="black")
```

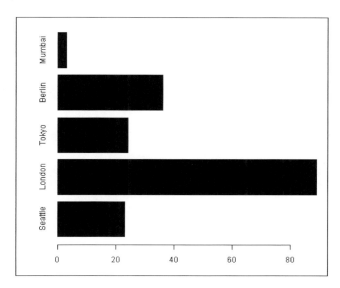

How it works...

The first argument of the `barplot()` function is either a vector or matrix of values which you want to plot as bars, such as the sales data variables in the examples we have just seen. The labels for the bars are specified by the `names.arg` argument, but we use this argument only when plotting single bars. In the example with sales figures for multiple products, we didn't specify `names.arg`. R automatically used the product names as the labels and we had to instead specify the city names as the legend.

As with the other types of plots, the `col` argument is used to specify the color of the bars. This is a common feature throughout R, that is `col` is used to set the color of the main feature in any kind of graph.

There's more...

Bar plots are often used to compare the values of groups of values across categories. For example, we can plot the sales in different cities for more than one product using the `beside` argument:

```
barplot(as.matrix(sales[,2:4]), beside=TRUE,
legend=sales$City,
col=heat.colors(5),
border="white")
```

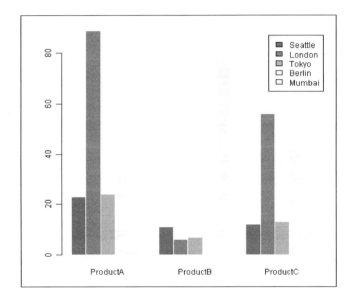

You will notice that when plotting data for multiple products (columns), we used the square bracket notation in the form `sales[,2:4]`. In R the square bracket notation is used to refer to specific columns and rows of a dataset. For example, `sales[2,3]` refers to the value in the second row and the third column.

So the notation is of the form `sales[row, column]`. If you want to refer to all the rows in a certain column you can omit the row number. For example, if you want to refer to all the rows in column two, you would use `sales[,2]`. Similarly, for all the columns of row three, you would use `sales[3,]`.

So `sales[,2:4]` refers to all the data in columns two to four, which is the product sales data as shown in the following table:

City	ProductA	ProductB	ProductC
San Francisco	23	11	12
London	89	6	56
Tokyo	24	7	13
Berlin	36	34	44
Mumbai	3	78	14

The orientation of bars is set to vertical by default. It is controlled by the optional `horiz` (for horizontal) argument. If we do not use this argument in our `barplot()` function call, it is set to `FALSE`. To make the bars horizontal, we set `horiz` to `TRUE`.

The `beside` argument is used to specify whether we want the bars in a group of data to be stacked or adjacent to each other. By default, `beside` is set to `FALSE`, which produces a stacked bar graph. To make the bars adjacent, we set `beside` to `TRUE`.

To change the color of the border around the bars. we used the `border` argument. The default border color is black. But if you wish to use another color, say white, you can set it with `border="white"`.

To make the same graph with horizontal bars we would type:

```
barplot(as.matrix(sales[,2:4]), beside=TRUE,
legend=sales$City,
col=heat.colors(5),
border="white",
horiz=TRUE)
```

See also

Bar charts will be explored in a lot more detail with some advanced recipes in *Chapter 5, Creating Bar, Dot, and Pie Charts*.

Creating histograms and density plots

In this recipe, we will learn how to make histograms and density plots, which are useful to look at the distribution of values in a dataset.

How to do it...

The simplest way to demonstrate the use of a histogram is to show a normal distribution:

```
hist(rnorm(1000))
```

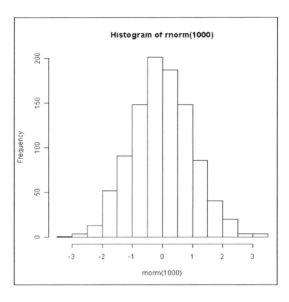

Another example of a histogram is one which shows a skewed distribution:

```
hist(islands)
```

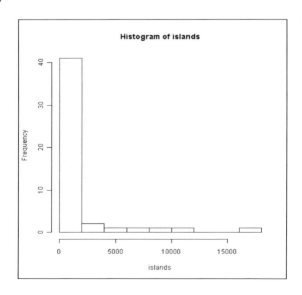

How it works...

The hist () function is also a function of R's base graphics library. It takes only one compulsory argument, that is the variable whose distribution of values we wish to visualize.

In the first example, we passed the rnorm () function as the variable. rnorm(1000) generates a vector of 1,000 random numbers with a normal distribution. As you can see in the histogram, it's a bell-shaped curve.

In the second example, we passed the inbuilt islands dataset (which gives the areas of the world's major landmasses) as the argument to hist (). As you can see from that histogram, islands has a distribution skewed heavily towards the lower value range of 0 to 2,000 square miles.

There's more...

As you may have noticed in the preceding examples, the default setting for histograms is to display the frequency or number of occurrences of values in a particular range on the Y axis. We can also display probabilities instead of frequencies by setting the prob (for probability) argument to TRUE or the freq (for frequency) argument to FALSE.

Now let's make a density plot for the same function rnorm (). To do so, we need to use the density () function and pass it as our first argument to plot () as follows:

```
plot(density(rnorm(1000)))
```

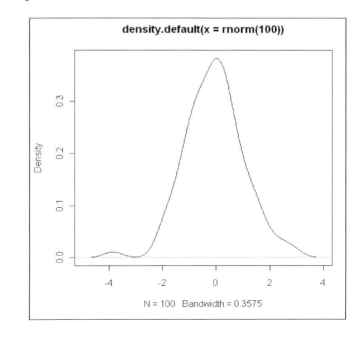

See also

We will cover more details such as setting the breaks, density, formatting of bars and other advanced recipes in *Chapter 6, Creating Histograms*.

Creating box plots

In this recipe, we will learn how to make box plots, which are useful in comparing the spread of values in different measurements.

Getting ready

First we need to load the `metals.csv` example data file, which contains measurements of metal concentrations in London's air. You can download this file from the code download section of the book's companion website:

```
metals<-read.csv("metals.csv",header=TRUE)
```

How to do it...

We can make a box plot to summarize the metal concentration data using the `boxplot()` command as follows:

```
boxplot(metals,
xlab="Metals",
ylab="Atmospheric Concentration in ng per cubic metre",
main="Atmospheric Metal Concentrations in London")
```

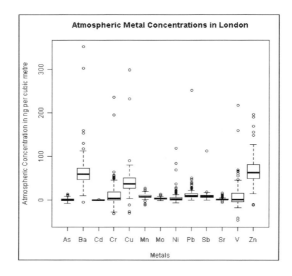

How it works...

The main argument a `boxplot()` function takes is a set of numeric values (in the form of a vector or data frame). In our first example, we used a dataset containing numerical values of air pollution data from London. The dark line inside the box for each metal represents the median of values for that metal. The bottom and top edges of the box represent the first and third quartiles respectively. Thus, the length of the box is equal to the interquartile range (IQR, difference between first and third quartiles). The maximum length of a whisker is a multiple of the IQR (default multiplier is approximately 1.5). The ends of the whiskers are at data points closest to the maximum length of the whisker.

All the points lying beyond these whiskers are considered outliers.

As with most other plot types, the common arguments such as `xlab`, `ylab`, and `main` can be used to set the titles for the X and Y axes and the graph itself respectively.

There's more...

We can also make another type of box plot where we can group the observations by categories. For example, if we want to study the spread of copper concentrations by the source of the measurements, we can use a formula to include the source. First we need to read the `copper_site.csv` example data file, as follows:

```
copper<-read.csv("copper_site.csv",header=TRUE)
```

Then we can add the following code:

```
boxplot(copper$Cu~copper$Source,
xlab="Measurement Site",
ylab="Atmospheric Concentration of Copper in ng per cubic metre",
main="Atmospheric Copper Concentrations in London")
```

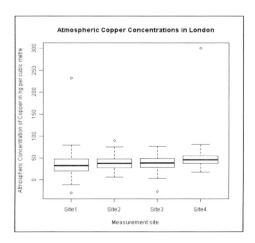

In this example, the `boxplot()` function takes a formula as an argument. This formula in the form `value~group (Cu~source)` specifies a column of values and the group of categories it should be summarized over.

See also

More detailed box plot recipes will be presented in *Chapter 7, Creating Box and Whisker Plots*.

Adjusting X and Y axes limits

In this recipe, we will learn how to adjust the X and Y limits of plots, which is useful in adjusting a graph to suit one's presentation needs and adding additional data to the same plot.

How to do it...

We will modify our first scatter plot example to demonstrate how to adjust axes limits:

```
plot(cars$dist~cars$speed,
xlim=c(0,30),
ylim=c(0,150))
```

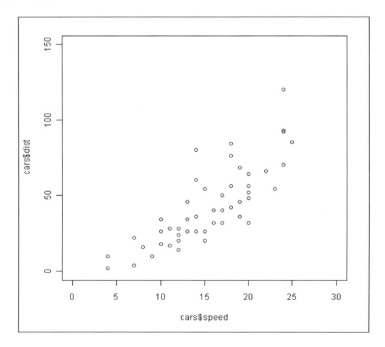

How it works...

In our original scatter plot in the first recipe of this chapter, the x axis limits were set to just below 5 and up to 25 and the y axis limits were set from 0 to 120. In this example, we set the x axis limit to 0 to 30 and y axis limits to 0 to 150 using the `xlim` and `ylim` arguments respectively.

Both `xlim` and `ylim` take a vector of length 2 as valid values in the form `c(minimum, maximum)` that is, `xlim=c(0,30)` means set the x axis minimum limit to 0 and maximum limit to 30.

There's more...

You may have noticed that even after setting the x and y limit values, there is some gap left at either edges. The two axes zeroes don't coincide. This is because R automatically adds some additional space at both the edges of the axes, so that if there are any data points at the extremes, they are not cut off by the axes. If you wish to set the axes limits to exact values, in addition to specifying `xlim` and `ylim`, you must also set the `xaxs` and `yaxs` arguments to `"i"`:

```
plot(cars$dist~cars$speed,
xlim=c(0,30),
ylim=c(0,150),
xaxs="i",
yaxs="i")
```

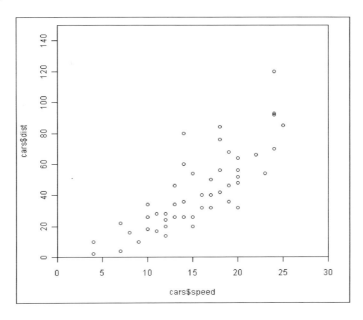

Sometimes, we may wish to reverse a data axis, say to plot the data in descending order along one axis. All we have to do is swap the minimum and maximum values in the vector argument supplied as `xlim` or `ylim`. So, if we want the X axis speed values in the previous graph in descending order we need to set `xlim` to `c(30,0)`:

```
plot(cars$dist~cars$speed,
xlim=c(30,0),
ylim=c(0,150),
xaxs="i",
yaxs="i")
```

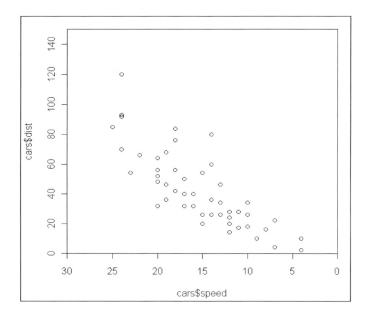

See also

There will be a few more recipes on adjusting the axes tick marks and labels in *Chapter 2, Beyond the Basics*.

Creating heat maps

Heat maps are colorful images, which are very useful for summarizing a large amount of data by highlighting hotspots or key trends in the data.

How to do it...

There are a few different ways to make heat maps in R. The simplest is to use the `heatmap()` function in the base library:

```
heatmap(as.matrix(mtcars),
Rowv=NA,
Colv=NA,
col = heat.colors(256),
scale="column",
margins=c(2,8),
main = "Car characteristics by Model")
```

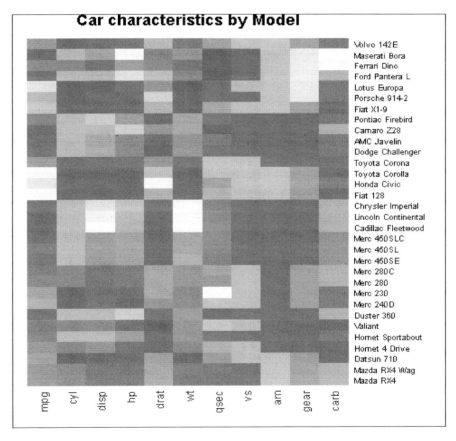

How it works...

The example code has a lot of arguments, so it may look difficult at first sight. But if we consider each argument in turn, we can understand how it works. The first argument to the `heatmap()` function is the dataset. We are using the inbuilt dataset `mtcars`, which holds data such as fuel efficiency (`mpg`), number of cylinders (`cyl`), weight (`wt`), and so on for different models of cars. The data needs to be in a matrix format, so we use the `as.matrix()` function. `Rowv` and `Colv` specify if and how dendrograms should be displayed to the left and top of the heat map.

 See `help(dendrogram)` and `http://en.wikipedia.org/wiki/Dendrogram` for details on dendrograms.

In our example, we suppress them by setting the two arguments to `NA`, which is a logical indicator of a missing value in R. The `scale` argument tells R in what direction the color gradient should apply. We have set it to column, which means the scale for the gradient will be calculated on a per-column basis.

There's more...

Heat maps are very useful for looking at correlations between variables in a large dataset. For example, in bioinformatics, heat maps are often used to study the correlations between groups of genes.

Let's look at an example with the `genes.csv` example data file. Let's first load the file:

```
genes<-read.csv("genes.csv",header=T)
```

Let's use the `image()` function to create a correlation heat map:

```
rownames(genes)<-colnames(genes)

image(x=1:ncol(genes),
y=1:nrow(genes),
z=t(as.matrix(genes)),
axes=FALSE,
xlab="",
ylab="" ,
main="Gene Correlation Matrix")

axis(1,at=1:ncol(genes),labels=colnames(genes),col="white",
las=2,cex.axis=0.8)
axis(2,at=1:nrow(genes),labels=rownames(genes),col="white",
las=1,cex.axis=0.8)
```

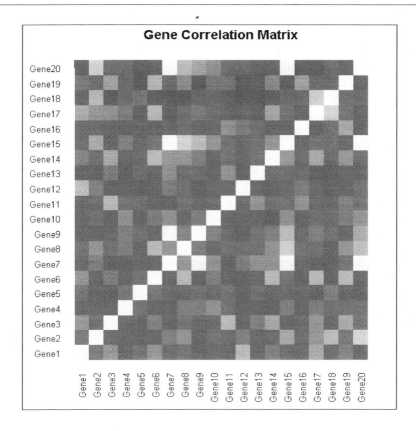

We have used a few new commands and arguments in this example, especially for formatting the axes. We will discuss these in detail starting in *Chapter 2, Beyond the Basics* and with more examples in later chapters.

See also

Heat maps will be explained in a lot more detail with more examples in *Chapter 8, Creating Heat Maps*.

Creating pairs plots

A pairs plot is a matrix of scatter plots which is a very handy visualization for quickly scanning the correlations between many variables in a dataset.

How to do it...

We will use the inbuilt `iris` dataset, which gives the measurements in centimeters of the variables sepal length, sepal width, petal length and petal width, respectively, for 50 flowers from each of three species of iris:

```
pairs(iris[,1:4])
```

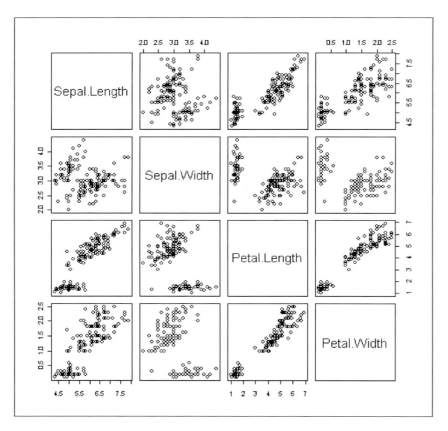

How it works...

As you can see in the figure, the `pairs()` command makes a matrix of scatter plots, where all the variables in the specified dataset are plotted against each other. The variable names, displayed in the diagonal running across from the top left to the bottom right, are the key to reading the graph. For example, the scatter plot in the first row and second column shows the relationship between **Sepal Length** on the Y axis and **Sepal Width** on the X axis.

There's more...

Here's a fun fact: we can produce the previous graph using the `plot()` function instead of `pairs()` in exactly the same manner:

```
plot(iris[,1:4],
main="Relationships between characteristics of iris flowers",
pch=19,
col="blue",
cex=0.9)
```

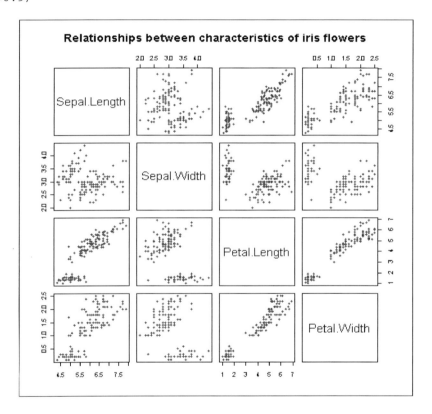

So if you pass a data frame with more than two variables to the `plot()` function, it creates a scatter plot matrix by default. We've also added a plot title and modified the plotting symbol style, color and size using the `pch`, `col` and `cex` arguments respectively. We'll delve into the details of these settings in *Chapter 2, Beyond the Basics*.

See also

We'll cover some more interesting recipes in *Chapter 3*, *Creating Scatter Plots*, building upon the things we learn in *Chapter 2*.

Creating multiple plot matrix layouts

In this recipe, we will learn how to present more than one graph in a single image. Pairs plots are one example as we saw in the last recipe, but here we will learn how to include different types of graphs in each cell of a graph matrix.

How to do it...

Let's say we want to make a 2x3 matrix of graphs, made of two rows and three columns of graphs. We use the par() command as follows:

```
par(mfrow=c(2,3))
plot(rnorm(100),col="blue",main="Plot No.1")
plot(rnorm(100),col="blue",main="Plot No.2")
plot(rnorm(100),col="green",main="Plot No.3")
plot(rnorm(100),col="black",main="Plot No.4")
plot(rnorm(100),col="green",main="Plot No.5")
plot(rnorm(100),col="orange",main="Plot No.6")
```

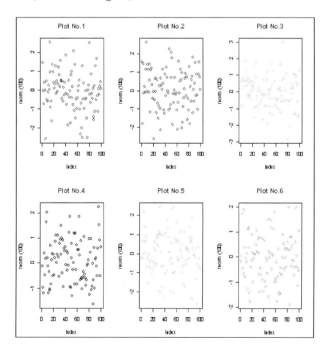

How it works...

The `par()` command is by far the most important function for customizing graphs in R. It is used to set and query many graphical arguments (hence par), which control the layout and appearance of graphs.

Please note that we need to issue the `par()` command *before* the actual graph commands. When you first run the `par()` command, only a blank graphics window appears. The `par()` command sets the argument for any subsequent graphs made. The `mfrow` argument is used to specify how many rows and columns of graphs we wish to plot. The `mfrow` argument takes values in the form of a vector of length two: `c(nrow,ncol)`. The first number specifies the number of rows and the second specifies the number of columns. In our previous example, we wanted a matrix of two rows and three columns, so we set `mfrow` to `c(2,3)`.

Note that there is another argument `mfcol`, similar to `mfrow`, which can also be used to create multiple plot layouts. `mfcol` also takes a two value vector specifying the number of rows and columns in the matrix. The difference is that `mfcol` draws subsequent figures by columns, rather than by rows as `mfrow` does. So, if we used `mfcol` instead of `mfrow` in the earlier example, we would get the following plot:

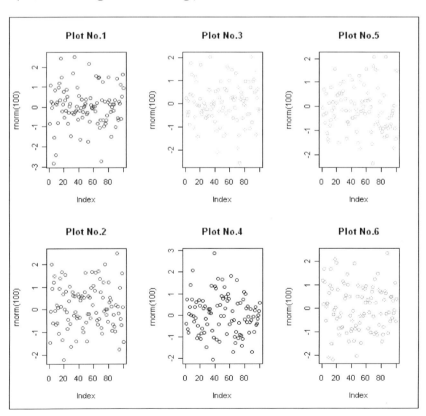

There's more...

Let's look at a practical example where a multiple plot layout would be useful. Let's read the `dailymarket.csv` example file that contains data on the daily revenue, profits, and number of customer visits for a shop:

```
market<-read.csv("dailymarket.csv",header=TRUE)
```

Now, let's plot all the three variables over time in a plot matrix with the graphs stacked over one another:

```
par(mfrow=c(3,1))

plot(market$revenue~as.Date(market$date,"%d/%m/%y"),
type="l", #Specify type of plot as l for line
main="Revenue",
xlab="Date",
ylab="US Dollars",
col="blue")

plot(market$profits~as.Date(market$date,"%d/%m/%y"),
type="l", #Specify type of plot as l for line
main="Profits",
xlab="Date",
ylab="US Dollars",
col="red")

plot(market$customers~as.Date(market$date,"%d/%m/%y"),
type="l", #Specify type of plot as l for line
main="Customer visits",
xlab="Date",
ylab="Number of people",
col="black")
```

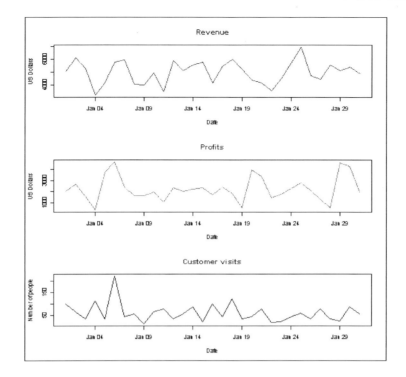

The preceding graph is a good way to visualize variables with different value ranges over the same time period. It helps in identifying where the trends match each other and where they differ.

See also

We will explore more examples and uses of multiple plot layouts in later chapters.

Adding and formatting legends

In this recipe, we will learn how to add and format legends to graphs.

Getting ready

First we need to load the `cityrain.csv` example data file, which contains monthly rainfall data for four major cities across the world. You can download this file from the code download section of the book's companion website:

```
rain<-read.csv("cityrain.csv",header=TRUE)
```

How to do it...

In the bar plots recipe, we already saw that we can add a legend by passing the `legend` argument to the `barplot()` function. Now we see how we can use the `legend()` function to add and customize a legend for any type of graph.

Let's first draw a graph with multiple lines representing the rainfall in cities:

```
plot(rain$Tokyo,type="l",col="red",
ylim=c(0,300),
main="Monthly Rainfall in major cities",
xlab="Month of Year",
ylab="Rainfall (mm)",
lwd=2)
lines(rain$NewYork,type="l",col="blue",lwd=2)
lines(rain$London,type="l",col="green",lwd=2)
lines(rain$Berlin,type="l",col="orange",lwd=2)
```

Now let's add the legend to mark which line represents which city:

```
legend("topright",
legend=c("Tokyo","NewYork","London","Berlin"),
col=c("red","blue","green","orange"),
lty=1,lwd=2)
```

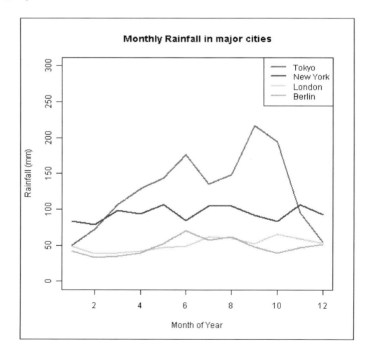

How it works...

In the example code, we first created a graph with multiple lines using the `plot()` and `lines()` commands to represent the monthly rainfall in Tokyo, New York, London, and Berlin in four different colors. However, without a legend one would have no way of telling which line represents which city. So we added a legend using the `legend()` function.

The first argument to the `legend()` function is the position of the legend, which we set to `topright`. Other possible values are `"topleft"`, `"top"`, `"left"`, `"center"`, `"right"`, `"bottomleft"`, `"bottom"`, and `"bottomright"`. Then we specify the legend labels by setting the `legend` argument to a vector of length 4 containing the names of the four cities. The `col` argument specifies the colors of the legend, which should match the colors of the lines in exactly the same order. Finally, the line type and width inside the legend are specified by `lty` and `lwd` respectively.

There's more...

The placement and look of the legend can be modified in several ways. As a simple example, let's spread the legend across the top of the graph instead of the top right corner. So first, let's redraw the same base plot:

```
plot(rain$Tokyo,type="l",col="red",
ylim=c(0,250),
main="Monthly Rainfall in major cities",
xlab="Month of Year",
ylab="Rainfall (mm)",
lwd=2)
lines(rain$NewYork,type="l",col="blue",lwd=2)
lines(rain$London,type="l",col="green",lwd=2)
lines(rain$Berlin,type="l",col="orange",lwd=2)
```

Now, let's add a modified legend:

```
legend("top",
legend=c("Tokyo","NewYork","London","Berlin"),
ncol=4,
cex=0.8,
bty="n",
col=c("red","blue","green","orange"),
lty=1,lwd=2)
```

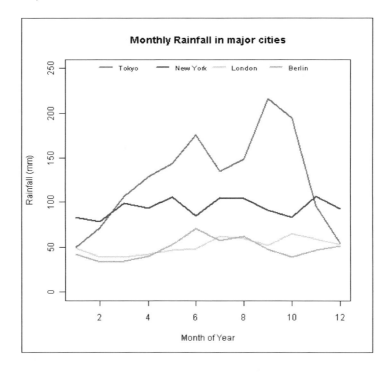

We changed the legend location from `topright` to `top` and added a few other arguments to adjust the look. The `ncol` argument is used to specify the number of columns over which the legend is displayed. The default value is `1` as we saw in the first example. In our second example, we set `ncol` to `4` so that all the city names are displayed in one single row. The argument `bty` specifies the type of box drawn around the legend. We removed it from the graph by setting it to `"n"`. We also modified the size of the legend labels by setting `cex` to `0.8`.

See also

There are plenty of examples of how you can add and customize legends in different scenarios in later chapters.

Creating graphs with maps

In this recipe, we will learn how to plot data on maps.

Getting ready

In order to plot maps in R, we need to install the maps library. Here's how to do it:

```
install.packages("maps")
```

When you run this command, you will most likely be prompted by R to choose from a list of locations from where you can download the library. For example, if you are based in the UK, you can choose either the **UK (Bristol)** or **UK (London)** options.

Once the library is installed, we must load it using the `library()` command:

```
library(maps)
```

 Note that we need to install any package using `install.packages()` only once but need to load it using `library()` or `require()` every time we restart a new session in R.

How to do it...

We can make a simple world map with just one command:

```
map()
```

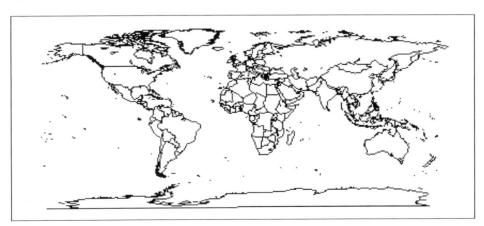

Let's add color:

```
map('world', fill = TRUE,col=heat.colors(10))
```

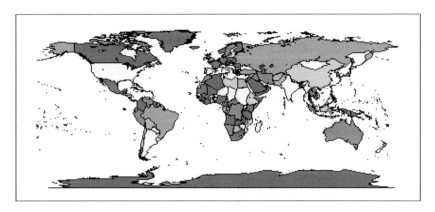

How it works...

The `maps` library provides a way to project world data on to a low resolution map. It is also possible to make detailed maps of the United States. For example, we can make a map showing the state boundaries as follows:

```
map("state", interior = FALSE)
map("state", boundary = FALSE, col="red", add = TRUE)
```

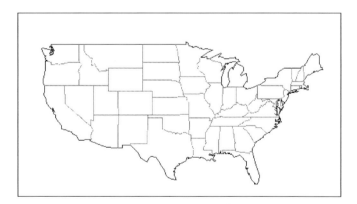

The `add` argument is set to `TRUE` in the second call to `map()` to add details to the same map created using the first call. It only works if a map has already been drawn on the current graphic device.

There's more...

The previous examples are just a basic introduction to the idea of geographical visualization in R. In order to plot any useful data, we need to use a better maps library. **GADM** (`http://gadm.org`) is a free spatial database of the location of the world's administrative areas (or administrative boundaries). The site provides map information as native R objects that can be plotted directly with the use of the `sp` library.

Let's take a look at a quick example. First we need to install and load the `sp` library, just like we did with the `maps` library:

```
install.packages("sp")
library(sp)
```

GADM provides data for all the countries across the world. Let's load the data for Great Britain. We can do so by directly reading the data from the GADM website:

```
load(url("http://gadm.org/data/rda/GBR_adm1.RData"))
```

This command loads the boundary data for the group of administrative regions forming Great Britain. It is stored in memory as a data object named `gadm`. Now let's plot a map with the loaded data:

```
spplot(gadm, "Shape_Area")
```

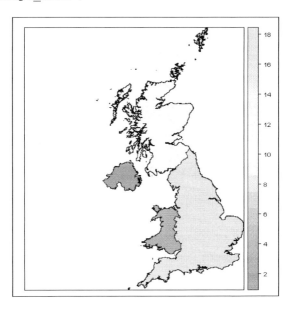

The graph shows the different parts of Great Britain, color coded by their surface areas. We could just as easily display any other data such as population or crime rates.

See also

We will cover more detailed and practical recipes with maps in *Chapter 9, Creating Maps*.

Saving and exporting graphs

In this recipe, we will learn how to save and export our graphs to various useful formats.

How to do it...

To save a graph as an image file format such as PNG, we can use the png() command:

```
png("scatterplot.png")
plot(rnorm(1000))
dev.off()
```

The preceding command will save the graph as scatterplot.png in the current working directory. Similarly, if we wish to save the graph as JPEG, BMP or TIFF we can use the jpeg(), bmp(), or tiff() commands respectively.

If you are working under Windows, you can also save a graph using the graphical user interface. First make your graph, make sure the graph window is the active window by clicking anywhere inside it and then click on **File | Save as | Png** or the format of your choice as shown in the following screenshot:

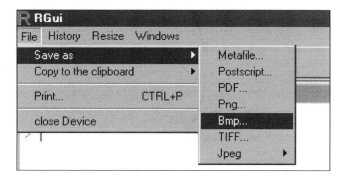

When prompted to choose a name for your saved file, type a suitable name and click **Save**. As you can see, you can choose from 7 different formats.

How it works...

If you wish to use code to save and export your graphs, it is important to understand how the code works. The first step in saving a graph is to open a graphics device suitable for the format of your choice before you make the graph. For example, when you call the png() function, you are telling R to start the PNG graphics device, such that the output of any subsequent graph commands you run will be directed to that device. By default, the display device on the screen is active. So any graph commands result in showing the graph on your screen. But you will notice that when you choose a different graphics device such as png(), the graphs don't show up on your screen. Finally, you must close the graphics device with the dev.off() command to instruct R to save the graph you plotted in the specified format and write it to disk with the specified filename. If you do not run dev.off(), the file will not be saved.

There's more...

You can specify a number of arguments to adjust the graph as per your needs. The simplest one that we've already used is the filename. You can also adjust the height and width settings of the graph:

```
png("scatterplot.png",
height=600,
width=600)
```

The default units for height and width are pixels but you can also specify the units in inches, cm or mm:

```
png("scatterplot.png",
height=4,
width=4,
units="in")
```

The resolution of the saved image can be specified in dots per inch (dpi) using the res argument:

```
png("scatterplot.png",
res=600)
```

If you want your graphs saved in a vector format, you can also save them as a PDF file using the pdf() function:

```
pdf("scatterplot.pdf")
```

Besides maintaining a high resolution of your graphs independent of size, PDFs are also useful because you can save multiple graphs in the same PDF file.

See also

We will cover the details of saving and exporting graphs, especially for publication and presentation purposes in *Chapter 10*.

2
Beyond the Basics: Adjusting Key Parameters

In this chapter, we will cover:

- ▶ Setting colors of points, lines, and bars
- ▶ Setting plot background colors
- ▶ Setting colors for text elements: axis annotations, labels, plot titles, and legends
- ▶ Choosing color combinations and palettes
- ▶ Setting fonts for annotations and titles
- ▶ Choosing plotting point symbol styles and sizes
- ▶ Choosing line styles and width
- ▶ Choosing box styles
- ▶ Adjusting axis annotations and tick marks
- ▶ Formatting log axes
- ▶ Setting graph margins and dimensions

Introduction

In this chapter, we will learn about some of the simplest yet most important settings and parameters of graphs in R base graphics. Learning how to adjust colors, sizes, margins, and styles of various graph elements such as points, lines, bars, axes, and titles will give us the ability to improve upon the basic graph commands we learnt in *Chapter 1*.

In the previous chapter, we got a glimpse of the different types of graphs that can be made in R using small snippets of code. Now, we will learn how to modify the fundamental building blocks of those graphs to better suit our needs.

The R base library has very powerful graphical capabilities. While you can produce pretty much any type of graph with a couple of lines of code, the default layout and look of the graph is often very basic. Sometimes, you may run into problems such as axis labels and titles getting chopped off at the edges or the legend size or position may mask part of your graph. Sometimes, the default color combinations may not be suitable for presentation or publication.

In this chapter we will go through the relevant names and accepted values of different arguments and arguments to graph functions. We will take a closer look at the `par()` function, which we briefly introduced in the previous chapter.

Reading and trying out all the recipes in this chapter is highly recommended as it will give you a very good hands-on grasp of certain aspects of graph manipulation, which you are likely to use a lot in any visual analysis in R.

Let's get started!

Setting colors of points, lines, and bars

In this recipe we will learn the simplest way to change the colors of points, lines, and bars in scatter plots, line plots, histograms, and bar plots.

Getting ready

All you need to try out this recipe is to run R and type the recipe at the command prompt. You can also choose to save the recipe as a script so that you can use it again later on.

How to do it...

The simplest way to change the color of any graph element is by using the `col` argument. For example, the `plot()` function takes the `col` argument:

```
plot(rnorm(1000),
col="red")
```

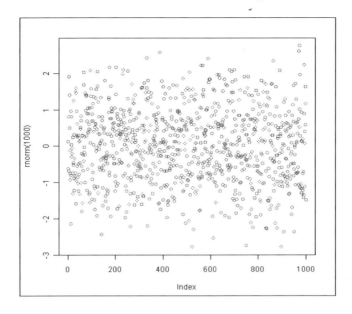

If we choose plot type as line, then the color is applied to the plotted line. Let's use the `dailysales.csv` example dataset we used in *Chapter 1*. First, we need to load it:

```
Sales <- read.csv("dailysales.csv",header=TRUE)

plot(sales$units~as.Date(sales$date,"%d/%m/%y"),
type="l", #Specify type of plot as l for line
col="blue")
```

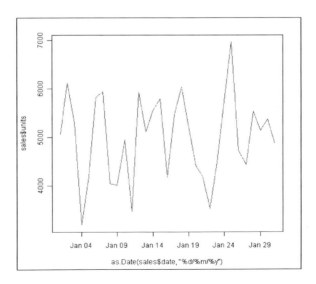

Similarly, the `points()` and `lines()` functions apply the `col` argument's value to the plotted points and lines respectively.

`barplot()` and `hist()` also take the `col` argument and apply them to the bars. So the following code would produce a bar plot with blue bars:

```
barplot(sales$ProductA~sales$City,
col="blue")
```

The `col` argument for `boxplot()` is applied to the color of the boxes plotted.

How it works...

The `col` argument automatically applies the specified color to the elements being plotted, based on the plot type. So, if we do not specify a plot type or choose points, then the color is applied to points. Similarly, if we choose plot type as line then the color is applied to the plotted line and if we use the `col` argument in the `barplot()` or `histogram()` commands, then the color is applied to the bars.

`col` accepts names of colors such as `red`, `blue`, and `black`. The `colors()` (or `colours()`) function lists all the built-in colors (more than 650) available in R. We can also specify colors as hexadecimal codes such as `#FF0000` (for red), `#0000FF` (for blue), and `#000000` (for black). If you have ever made any web pages, you would know that these hex codes are used in HTML to represent colors.

`col` can also take numeric values. When it is set to a numeric value, the color corresponding to that index in the current color palette is used. For example, in the default color palette the first color is black and the second color is red. So `col=1` and `col=2` refers to black and red respectively. Index `0` corresponds to the background color.

There's more...

In many settings, `col` can also take a vector of multiple colors, instead of a single color. This is useful if you wish to use more than one color in a graph. For example, in *Chapter 1* we made a bar plot of sales data for three products across five cities. In that example, we did use a vector of five colors to represent each of the five cities with the help of the `heat.colors()` function. The `heat.colors()` function takes a number as an argument and returns a vector of those many colors. So `heat.colors(5)` produces a vector of five colors.

Type the following at the R prompt:

```
heat.colors(5)
```

You should get the following output:

```
[1] "#FF0000FF" "#FF5500FF" "#FFAA00FF" "#FFFF00FF" "#FFFF80FF"
```

Those are five colors in the hexadecimal format.

Another way of specifying a vector of colors is to construct one:

```
barplot(as.matrix(sales[,2:4]), beside=T,
legend=sales$City,
col=c("red","blue","green","orange","pink"),
border="white")
```

In the example, we set the value of col to c("red","blue","green","orange", "pink"), which is a vector of five colors.

We have to take care to make a vector matching the length of the number of elements, in this case bars we are plotting. If the two numbers don't match, R will 'recycle' values by repeating colors from the beginning of the vector. For example, if we had fewer colors in the vector than the number of elements, say if we had four colors in the previous plot, then R would apply the four colors to the first four bars and then apply the first color to the fifth bar. This is called recycling in R:

```
barplot(as.matrix(sales[,2:4]), beside=T,
legend=sales$City,
col=c("red","blue","green","orange"),
border="white")
```

In the example, both the bars for the first and last data rows (**Seattle** and **Mumbai**) would be of the same color (red), making it difficult to distinguish one from the other.

One good way to ensure that you always have the correct number of colors is to find out the length of the number of elements first and pass that as an argument to one of the color palette functions. For example, if we did not know the number of cities in the example we have just seen; we could do the following to make sure the number of colors matches the number of bars plotted:

```
barplot(as.matrix(sales[,2:4]), beside=T,
legend=sales$City,
col=heat.colors(length(sales$City)),
border="white")
```

We used the length() function to find out the length or the number of elements in the vector sales$City and passed that as the argument to heat.colors(). So, regardless of the number of cities we will always have the right number of colors.

See also

In the next four recipes, we will see how to change the colors of other elements. The fourth recipe is especially useful where we look at color combinations and palettes.

Setting plot background colors

The default background color of all plots in R is white, which is usually the best choice as it is least distracting for data analysis. However, sometimes we may wish to use another color. We will see how to set background colors in this recipe.

Getting ready

All you need to try out this recipe is to run R and type the recipe at the command prompt. You can also choose to save the recipe as a script so that you can use it again later on.

How to do it...

To set the plot background color to gray we use the bg argument in the par() command:

```
par(bg="gray")
plot(rnorm(100))
```

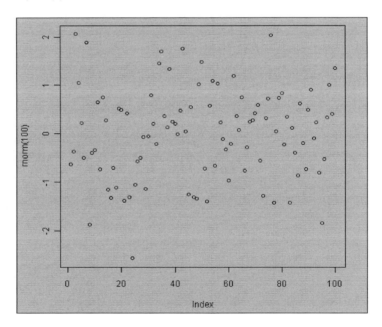

How it works...

The par() command's bg argument sets the background color for the entire plotting area including the margins for any subsequent plots on the same device. Until the plotting device is closed or a new device is initiated, the background color stays the same.

There's more...

It is more likely that we want to set the background color only for the plot region (within the axes) but there is no straightforward way to do this in R. We must draw a rectangle of the desired color in the background and then make our graph on top of it:

```
plot(rnorm(1000),type="n")
x<-par("usr")
rect(x[1],x[3],x[2],x[4],col="lightgray ")
points(rnorm(1000))
```

First we draw the plot with `type` set to "n" so that the plotted elements are invisible. This does not show the graph points or lines but sets the axes up, which we need for the next step.

`par("usr")` gets us the co-ordinates of the plot region in a vector of form `c(xleft, xright, ybottom, ytop)`. We then use the `rect()` function to draw a rectangle with a fill color that we wish to use for the plot background. Note that `rect()` takes a set of arguments representing the `xleft, ybottom, xright, ytop` co-ordinates. So we must pass the values we obtained from `par("usr")` in the correct order. Then, finally we redraw the graph with the correct type (points or lines).

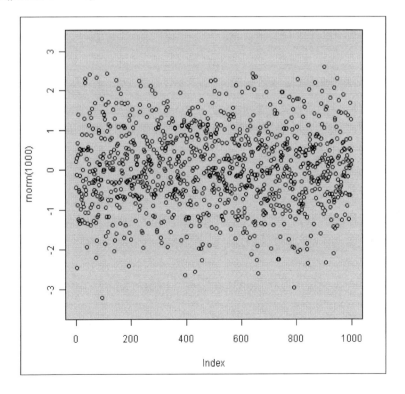

Setting colors for text elements: axis annotations, labels, plot titles, and legends

Axis annotations are the numerical or text values placed beside tick marks on an axis. Axis labels are the names or titles of axes, which tell the reader what the values on a particular axis represent. In this recipe, we will learn how to set the colors for these elements and legends.

Getting ready

All you need to try out this recipe is to run R and type the recipe at the command prompt. You can also choose to save the recipe as a script so that you can use it again later on.

How to do it...

Let's say we want to make the axis value annotations black, the labels of the axes gray, and the plot title dark blue, you should do the following:

```
plot(rnorm(100),
main="Plot Title",
col.axis="blue",
col.lab="red",
col.main="darkblue")
```

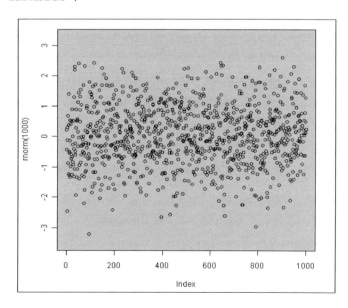

How it works...

Colors for axis annotations, labels, and plot titles can be set either using the `par()` command before making the graph or in the graph command such as `plot()` itself. The arguments for setting the colors for axis annotations, labels, and plot titles are `col.axis`, `col.lab`, and `col.main` respectively.

They are similar to the `col` argument and take names of colors or hex codes as values, but do not take a vector of more than one color.

There's more...

If we use the `par()` command, the difference is that `par()` will apply these settings to every subsequent graph, until it is reset either by specifying the settings again or starting a new graphics device:

```
par(col.axis="black",
col.lab="#444444",
col.main="darkblue")

plot(rnorm(100),main="plot")
```

The `col.axis` argument can also be passed to the `axis()` function, which is useful for making a custom axis if you do not want to use the default axis. The `col.lab` argument does not work with `axis()` and must be specified in `par()` or the main graph function such as `plot()` or `barplot()`.

The `col.main` argument can also be passed to the `title()` function, which is useful for adding a custom plot title if you do not want to use the default title:

```
title("Sales Figures for 2010", col.main="blue")
```

Axis labels can also be specified with `title()`:

```
title(xlab="Month",ylab="Sales",col.lab="red")
```

This is handy because you can specify two different colors for the X and Y axes:

```
title(xlab="X axis",col.lab="red")
title(ylab="Y axis",col.lab="blue")
```

When setting the axis titles with the `title()` command, we must set `xlab` and `ylab` to empty strings "" in the original plot command to avoid overlapping titles.

Choosing color combinations and palettes

We often need more than one color to represent various elements in graphs. Palettes are combinations of colors which are a convenient way to use multiple colors without choosing individual colors separately. R provides inbuilt color palettes as well as the ability to make our own custom palettes. Using palettes is a good way to avoid repeatedly choosing or setting colors in multiple locations, which can be a source of error and confusion. It helps in separating the presentation settings of a graph from the construction.

Getting ready

All you need to try out this recipe is to run R and type the recipe at the command prompt. You can also choose to save the recipe as a script so that you can use it again later on. One new library needs to be installed, which is also explained.

How to do it...

We can change the current palette by passing a character vector of colors to the `palette()` function. For example:

```
palette(c("red","blue","green","orange"))
```

To use the colors in the current palette, we can refer to them by the index number. For example, `palette()[1]` would be `red`.

How it works...

R has a default palette of colors which can be accessed by calling the `palette()` function. If we run the `palette()` command just after starting R, we get the default palette:

```
palette()
[1] "black"    "red"      "green3"  "blue"    "cyan"    "magenta"
"yellow"
[8] "gray"
```

To revert back to the default palette type:

```
palette("default")
```

When a vector of color names is passed to the `palette()` function, it sets the current palette to those colors. We must enter valid color names otherwise we will get an invalid color name error.

There's more...

Besides the default palette provided by the `palette()` function, R has many more built-in palettes and additional palette libraries. One of the most commonly used palettes is the `heat.colors()` palette, which provides a range of colors from red through yellow to white, based on the number of colors specified by the argument n. For example, `heat.colors(10)` produces a palette of 10 warm colors from red to white.

Other palettes are `rainbow()`, `terrain.colors()`, `cm.colors()`, and `topo.colors` which take the number of colors as an argument.

`RColorBrewer` is a very good color palette package that creates nice looking color palettes especially for thematic maps. It is an R implementation of the `RColorBrewer` palettes, which provides three types of palettes: sequential, diverging, and qualitative. More information is available at `http://www.colorbrewer.org`.

To use `RColorBrewer`, we need to install and load it:

```
install.packages("RColorBrewer")
library(RColorBrewer)
```

To see all the `RColorBrewer` palettes run the following command at the R prompt:

```
display.brewer.all()
```

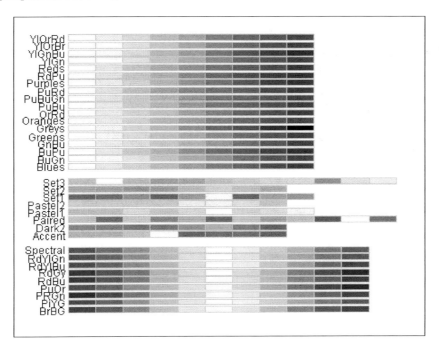

The names of the palettes are displayed in the left-hand margin and the colors in each palette are displayed in each row running to the right.

To use one of the palettes, let's say `YlOrRd` (which as the names suggests is a combination of yellows and reds), we can use the `brewer.pal()` function:

```
brewer.pal(7,"YlOrRd")
[1] "#FFFFB2" "#FED976" "#FEB24C" "#FD8D3C" "#FC4E2A" "#E31A1C"
"#B10026"
```

The `brewer.pal` function takes two arguments: the number of colors we wish to choose and the name of the palette. The minimum number of colors is three but the maximum varies from palette to palette.

We can view the colors of an individual palette by using the `display.brewer.pal()` command:

```
display.brewer.pal(7,"YlOrRd")
```

To use a specific color of the palette we can refer to it by its index number. So the first color in the palette is `brewer.pal(7,"YlOrRd")[1]`, the second is `brewer.pal(7,"YlOrRd")[2]`, and so on.

We can set the current palette to the previous one by using the `palette()` function:

```
palette(brewer.pal(7,"YlOrRd"))
```

Now we can refer to the individual colors as `palette()[1]`, `palette()[2]`, and so on. We can also store the palette as a vector:

```
pal1<- brewer.pal(7,"YlOrRd")
```

See also

We will see the use of a lot of color palettes throughout the recipes in this book starting from *Chapter 3, Creating Scatter Plots*.

Setting fonts for annotations and titles

For most data analysis we can just use the default fonts for titles. However, sometimes we may want to choose different fonts for presentation and publication purposes. Selecting fonts can be tricky as it depends on the operating system and the graphics device. We will see some simple ways to choose fonts in this recipe.

Getting ready

All you need to try out this recipe is to run R and type the recipe at the command prompt. You can also choose to save the recipe as a script so that you can use it again later on.

How to do it...

The font family and face can be set with the `par()` command:

```
par(family="serif",font=2)
```

How it works...

A font is specified in two parts: a font `family` (such as Helvetica or Arial) and a font `face` within that `family` (such as **bold** or *italic*).

The available font families vary by operating system and graphics devices. So R provides some proxy values which are mapped on to the relevant available fonts irrespective of the system. Standard values for family are "serif", "sans", and "mono".

The font argument takes numerical values: 1 corresponds to plain text (the default), 2 to bold face, 3 to italic, and 4 to bold italic.

For example, `par(family="serif",font=2)` sets the font to a bold Times New Roman on Windows. You can check the other font mappings by running the `windowsFonts()` command at the R prompt.

The fonts for axis annotations, labels, and plot main title can be set separately using the `font.axis`, `font.lab`, and `font.main` arguments respectively.

There's more...

The choice of fonts is very limited if we just use the proxy family names. However, we can use a wide range of fonts if we are exporting our graphs in the PostScript or PDF formats. The `postscriptFonts()` and `pdfFonts()` functions show all the available fonts for those devices. To see the PDF fonts, run the following command:

```
names(pdfFonts())
 [1] "serif"          "sans"                 "mono"
 [4] "AvantGarde"     "Bookman"              "Courier"
 [7] "Helvetica"      "Helvetica-Narrow"     "NewCenturySchoolbook"
[10] "Palatino"       "Times"                "URWGothic"
[13] "URWBookman"     "NimbusMon"            "NimbusSan"
```

```
[16] "URWHelvetica"      "NimbusSanCond"      "CenturySch"
[19] "URWPalladio"       "NimbusRom"          "URWTimes"
[22] "Japan1"            "Japan1HeiMin"       "Japan1GothicBBB"
[25] "Japan1Ryumin"      "Korea1"             "Korea1deb"
[28] "CNS1"              "GB1"
```

To use one of these font families in a PDF, we can pass the `family` argument to the `pdf()` function:

```
pdf(family="AvantGarde")  pdf(paste(family="AvantGarde")
```

See also

In *Chapter 10, Finalizing Graphs*, we will see some more practical recipes on setting fonts for publications and presentations.

Choosing plotting point symbol styles and sizes

In this recipe, we will see how we can adjust the styling of plotting symbols, which is useful and necessary when we plot more than one set of points representing different groups of data on the same graph.

Getting ready

All you need to try out this recipe is to run R and type the recipe at the command prompt. You can also choose to save the recipe as a script so that you can use it again later on. We will also use the `cityrain.csv` example data file that we used in the first chapter. Please read the file into R as follows:

```
rain<-read.csv("cityrain.csv")
```

How to do it...

The plotting symbol and size can be set using the `pch` and `cex` arguments:

```
plot(rnorm(100),pch=19,cex=2)
```

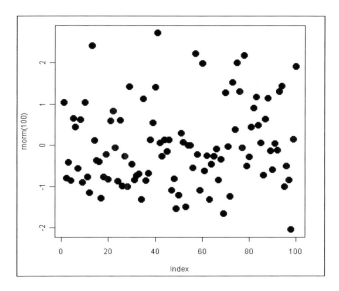

How it works...

The `pch` argument stands for plotting character (symbol). It can take numerical values (usually between 0 and 25) as well as single character values. Each numerical value represents a different symbol. For example, 1 represents circles, 2 represents triangles, 3 represents plus signs, and so on. If we set the value of `pch` to a character such as "*" or "£" in inverted commas, then the data points are drawn as that character instead of the default circles.

The size of the plotting symbol is controlled by the `cex` argument, which takes numerical values starting at 0 giving the amount by which plotting symbols should be magnified relative to the default. Note that `cex` takes relative values (the default is 1). So, the absolute size may vary depending on the defaults of the graphic device in use. For example, the size of plotting symbols with the same `cex` value may be different for a graph saved as a PNG file versus a graph saved as a PDF.

There's more...

The most common use of `pch` and `cex` is when we don't want to use color to distinguish between different groups of data points. This is often the case in scientific journals which do not accept color images. For example, let's plot the city rainfall data we looked at in *Chapter 1* as a set of points instead of lines:

```
plot(rain$Tokyo,
ylim=c(0,250),
main="Monthly Rainfall in major cities",
xlab="Month of Year",
```

```
ylab="Rainfall (mm)",
pch=1)

points(rain$NewYork,pch=2)
points(rain$London,pch=3)
points(rain$Berlin,pch=4)

legend("top",
legend=c("Tokyo","New York","London","Berlin"),
ncol=4,
cex=0.8,
bty="n",
pch=1:4)
```

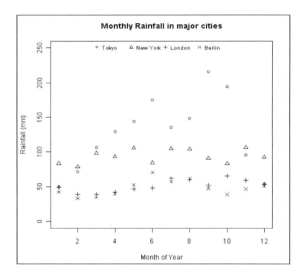

See also

We will see more examples of symbol settings later in the book, especially in the next chapter on scatter plots.

Choosing line styles and width

Similar to plotting point symbols, R provides simple ways to adjust the style of lines in graphs.

Getting ready

All you need to try out this recipe is to run R and type the recipe at the command prompt. You can also choose to save the recipe as a script so that you can use it again later on. We will again use the `cityrain.csv` data file that we read in the last recipe.

How to do it...

Line styles can be set by using the `lty` and `lwd` arguments (for line type and width respectively) in the `plot()`, `lines()`, and `par()` commands. Let's take our rainfall example and apply different line styles keeping the color the same:

```
plot(rain$Tokyo,
ylim=c(0,250),
main="Monthly Rainfall in major cities",
xlab="Month of Year",
ylab="Rainfall (mm)",
type="l",
lty=1,
lwd=2)

lines(rain$NewYork,lty=2,lwd=2)
lines(rain$London,lty=3,lwd=2)
lines(rain$Berlin,lty=4,lwd=2)

legend("top",
legend=c("Tokyo","New York","London","Berlin"),
ncol=4,
cex=0.8,
bty="n",
lty=1:4,
lwd=2)
```

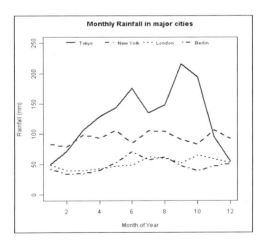

How it works...

Both line type and width can be set with numerical values as shown in the previous example. Line type number values correspond to types of lines:

- ▶ 0: `blank`
- ▶ 1: `solid` (default)
- ▶ 2: `dashed`
- ▶ 3: `dotted`
- ▶ 4: `dotdash`
- ▶ 5: `longdash`
- ▶ 6: `twodash`

We can also use the character strings instead of numbers, for example, `lty="dashed"` instead of `lty=2`.

The line width argument `lwd` takes positive numerical values. The default value is 1. In the example we used a value of 2, thus making the lines thicker than default.

See also

We will explore more examples of line styles in subsequent chapters, especially *Chapter 4, Creating Line Graphs and Time Series Charts* in which we will see some advanced line graph recipes.

Choosing box styles

The styles of various boxes drawn in a graph such as the one around the plotting region and the legend can be adjusted in a similar way to the line styles we saw in the last recipe.

Getting ready

All you need to try out this recipe is to run R and type the recipe at the command prompt. You can also choose to save the recipe as a script so that you can use it again later on.

How to do it...

Let's say we want to make an L-shaped box around a graph, such that the default top and right borders are not drawn. We can do so using the `bty` argument in the `par()` command:

```
par(bty="l")
plot(rnorm(100))
```

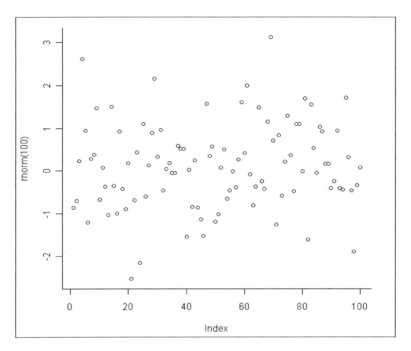

How it works...

The `bty` argument stands for box type and takes single characters in inverted commas as values. The resulting box resembles the corresponding upper case letter. For example, the default value is o, thus giving a box with all four edges. Other possible values are l, 7, c, u, and]. If we do not wish to draw a box at all, we can set `bty` to n.

Note that setting `bty` to n doesn't suppress the drawing of axes. If we wish to suppress those too then we would also have to set `xaxt` and `yaxt` to n. Alternatively, we can simply set the `axes` argument to `FALSE` in the `plot()` function call.

There's more...

Box styles can be controlled in a finer way using the box() command. In addition to the lty and lwd arguments, we can also specify where the box should be drawn using the which parameter, which can take values of plot, figure, inner, and outer.

Let's say we want to draw a graph with an L-shaped box for the plot area and a full box around the figure including the axis annotations and titles, then we can do:

```
par(oma=c(1,1,1,1))
plot(rnorm(100),bty="l")
box(which="figure")
```

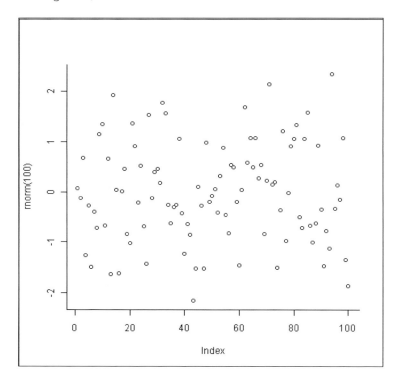

Note that we had to first set the outer margins by setting the oma argument with the par() function. We will learn more about this argument later in this chapter. If we did not set the outer margins, the box around the figure would be right at the edge of the plot and get cut off because the default margins are set to zero.

Adjusting axis annotations and tick marks

The default axis settings are often not adequate to deal with all kinds of data. For example, we may wish to change the number of tick marks along an axis or change the orientation of the annotations if they are too long to fit horizontally. In this recipe we will cover some settings which can be used to customize axes as per our requirements.

Getting ready

All you need to try out this recipe is to run R and type the recipe at the command prompt. You can also choose to save the recipe as a script so that you can use it again later on.

How to do it...

We can set the xaxp and yaxp arguments with the par() command to specify co-ordinates of the extreme tick marks and the number of intervals between tick marks in the form c(min,max,n).

```
plot(rnorm(100),xaxp=c(0,100,10))
```

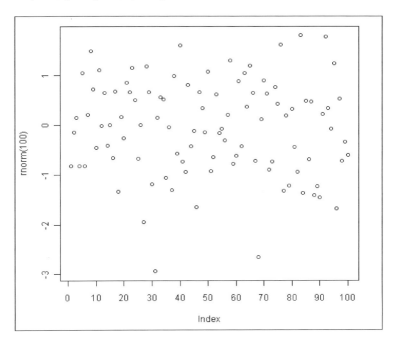

How it works...

When `xaxp` or `yaxp` is not specified, R automatically calculates the number of tick marks and their values. By default, R extends the axis limits by adding 4% at each end and then draws an axis which fits within the extended range. This means that even if we set the axis limits using `xlim` or `ylim`, the graph corners don't exactly correspond with those values. To make sure they do, we need to change the axis style using the `xaxs` argument, which takes one of two possible values: `r` (regular or default) and `i` (internal). We need to set `xaxs` to `i`.

A vector of the form `c(x1, x2, n)` giving the co-ordinates of the extreme tick marks and the number of intervals between tick marks

There's more...

To change the orientation of axis value annotations, we need to set the `las` argument of the `par()` command. It takes one of four possible numeric values:

- ▸ 0: always parallel to the axis (default)
- ▸ 1: always horizontal
- ▸ 2: always perpendicular to the axis
- ▸ 3: always vertical

We can also use the `axis()` command to make a custom axis by specifying a number of arguments. The basic arguments are:

- ▸ `side` which takes numeric values (1=below, 2=left, 3=above and 4=right)
- ▸ `at` which takes a vector of co-ordinates where tick marks are to be drawn
- ▸ `labels` which takes a vector of tick mark annotations

We can separately set the line width for the axis lines and the tick marks by passing the `lwd` and `lwd.ticks` arguments respectively. Similarly colors can be set using the `col` and `col.ticks` arguments.

See also

We will come across various examples of custom axes in the following chapters as we explore more advanced recipes.

Formatting log axes

In scientific analysis, we often need to represent data on a logarithmic scale. In this recipe, we will see how we can do this easily in R.

Getting ready

All you need to try out this recipe is to run R and type the recipe at the command prompt. You can also choose to save the recipe as a script so that you can use it again later on.

How to do it...

The simplest way to make an axes logarithmic is to use the log argument in the plot() command:

```
plot(10^c(1:5),log="y",type="b")
```

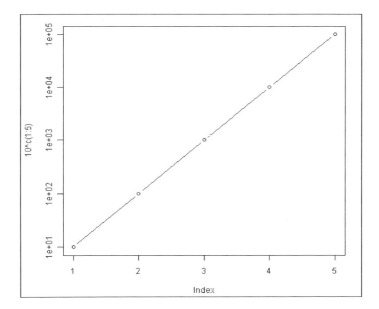

How it works...

The log argument takes character values specifying which axes should be logarithmic: x for X axis only, y for Y axis only, and xy or yx for both axes.

There's more...

We can also set scales to be logarithmic by setting the `xlog` and `ylog` arguments to TRUE with the `par()` command. This can be handy if we wish to have the same setting for multiple plots as `par()` applies the settings to all subsequent plots on the same device.

Note that R will not create the plot if our data contains zero or negative values.

Setting graph margins and dimensions

In this recipe we will learn how to adjust graph margins and dimensions.

Getting ready

All you need to try out this recipe is to run R and type the recipe at the command prompt. You can also choose to save the recipe as a script so that you can use it again later on.

How to do it...

We can use the `fin` and `pin` arguments of the `par()` command to set the figure region and plot dimensions:

```
par(fin=c(6,6),
pin=c(4,4))
```

We can use the `mai` and `omi` arguments to adjust the inner and outer margins respectively:

```
par(mai=c(1,1,1,1),
omi=c(0.1,0.1,0.1,0.1))
```

How it works...

All the previous arguments accept values in inches as a pair of width and height values. The default values for `fin` and `pin` are approximately 7x7 and 5.75x5.15. We have to be careful not to specify bigger values for `pin` than `fin` or we would get an error.

Adjusting `fin` and `pin` is one way of setting the figure margins containing the axis annotations and labels. Another way is to use the `mai` or `mar` arguments. In the example, we used `mai` which takes a vector value in inches, whereas `mar` takes a vector of numerical values in terms of number of lines of margins. It is better to use `mar` or `mai` because they adjust the figure margins irrespective of the figure or plot size.

We can also set an outer margin which is set to zero by default. This margin is useful if we wish to contain the entire graph including axis labels within a box as we saw in an earlier recipe. Like figure margins, outer margins can be set in inches with `omi` or in number of lines of text using `oma`.

R Graphics by Paul Murrell is an excellent reference with visual explanations of how margins work in R. See the book homepage for more details: `http://www.stat.auckland.ac.nz/~paul/RGraphics/rgraphics.html`.

This talk by Paul Murrell also contains figures from the book explaining the same concepts: `http://www.stat.auckland.ac.nz/~paul/Talks/Rgraphics.pdf`.

See also

We will come across examples of figure margin settings in some of the recipes in the following chapters.

3
Creating Scatter Plots

In this chapter, we will cover:

- ► Grouping data points within a scatter plot
- ► Highlighting grouped data points by size and symbol type
- ► Labelling data points
- ► Correlation matrix using pairs plot
- ► Adding error bars
- ► Using jitter to distinguish closely packed data points
- ► Adding linear model lines
- ► Adding non-linear model curves
- ► Adding non-parametric model curves with lowess
- ► Making three-dimensional scatter plots
- ► Making Quantile-Quantile plots
- ► Displaying data density on axes
- ► Making scatter plots with smoothed density representation

Introduction

In this chapter, we will learn about scatter plots in depth by looking at some advanced recipes. Scatter plots are one of the most commonly used type of graphs in data analysis. In the first chapter we learnt how to make a basic scatter plot. Now we will see how we can make more enhanced plots by adjusting various arguments and using some new functions.

So far, we have mostly only used the base graphics functions such as `plot()`, but in this chapter we have recipes that use other graph libraries such as `lattice` and `ggplot2`, which offer more advanced control over graphs. It is possible to make these advanced graphs using the base library too, but the additional libraries give us ways to achieve the same results with less code and often produce better looking graphs with the least amount of effort.

A lot of new functions will be introduced in this chapter. It is good practice to look up the help file whenever you encounter a new function. For example, to look up the help file for the `plot()` function, you can type `?plot` or `help(plot)` at the R command prompt.

As the recipes in this chapter are slightly more advanced than the earlier chapters, it may take some practice with multiple datasets before you are comfortable with using all the functions. Example datasets are used in each recipe, but it is highly recommended to also work with your own datasets and modify the recipes to suit your own analysis.

Grouping data points within a scatter plot

A basic scatter plot has a set of points plotted at the intersection of their values along X and Y axes. Sometimes, we may wish to further distinguish between these points based on another value associated with the points. In this recipe we will see how we can group data points using color.

Getting ready

To try out this recipe, start R and type the recipe at the command prompt. You can also choose to save the recipe as a script so that you can use it again later on.

We will also need the `lattice` and `ggplot2` packages. The `lattice` package is included automatically in the base R installation, but we will need to install the `ggplot2` package. To do this, run the following command at the R prompt:

```
install.packages("ggplot2")
```

How to do it...

As a first example, let's use the `xyplot()` command of the lattice library:

```
library(lattice)

xyplot(mpg~disp,
data=mtcars,
groups=cyl,
auto.key=list(corner=c(1,1)))
```

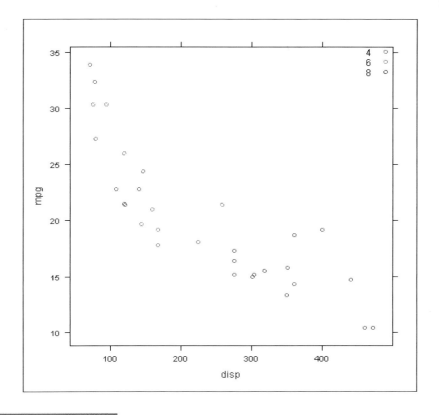

How it works...

In the example, we used the xyplot() command to plot **mpg** versus **disp** from the
pre-loaded mtcars dataset. We will understand this better if we look at the actual dataset.
Type mtcars at the R prompt and hit *Enter*. Let's look at a sample of the data to see the
row names and first three columns of data:

```
mtcars[1:6,1:3]
                    mpg    cyl    disp
Mazda RX4           21.0     6     160
Mazda RX4 Wag       21.0     6     160
Datsun 710          22.8     4     108
Hornet 4 Drive      21.4     6     258
Hornet Sportabout   18.7     8     360
Valiant             18.1     6     225
```

So we plotted `mpg` against `disp`, but we also used the `groups` argument to group the data points by `cyl`. That tells `xyplot()` that we would like to highlight the data points by different colors based on the number of cylinders (`cyl`) each car has. Finally, the `auto.key` argument is set to add a legend so that we know what values of `cyl` each color represents. The `auto.key` argument can take a list of values. The only one we have provided here is the location given by the corner argument, which we set to `c(1,1)` representing the top right corner. We can also simply set `auto.key` to `TRUE`, which will draw the legend in the top margin outside the plotting area.

There's more...

The `xyplot()` function has slightly obscure arguments. If you look at the help file on `xyplot()` (by running `?xyplot`), you will see that there are a lot of arguments which can be used to control many different aspects of the graph. A simpler alternative to `xyplot()` is using the functions from the `ggplot2` package. Let's draw the same plot using `ggplot2`:

```
library(ggplot2)
qplot(disp,mpg,data=mtcars,col= as.factor(cyl))
```

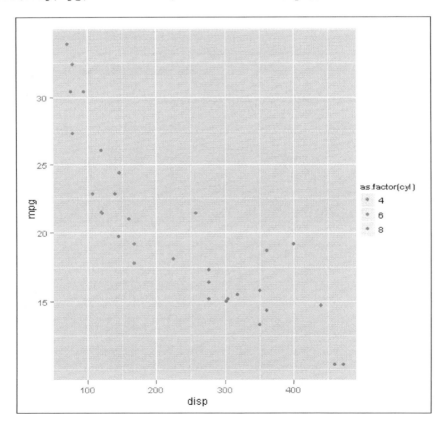

First we load the `ggplot2` library and then use the `qplot()` function to make the previous graph. We passed `disp` and `mpg` as the x and y variables respectively (note we can't use the y~x notation in qplot). To group by `cyl`, all we had to do was set the `col` argument to `cyl`. This tells `qplot` that we want to group the points based on the values of `cyl` and represent them by different colors. The legend is automatically drawn to the right.

Note that we set `col` to `as.factor(cyl)` and not just `cyl`. This is to make sure that `cyl` is read as a factor (or categorical value). If we just use `cyl`, then the plot is still the same, but the color scale and legend uses all the values between 4 and 8 as it takes `cyl` as a numerical variable.

Thus, it is easier and more intuitive to produce a better looking graph with `ggplot2`.

See also

We will use `ggplot2` to group data points by size and symbol instead of color in the next recipe.

Highlighting grouped data points by size and symbol type

Sometimes we may not want to use different colors to represent different groups of data points. For example, some journals accept graphs only in grayscale. In this recipe, we will see how we can highlight grouped data points by symbol size and type.

Getting ready

We will use the `ggplot2` library, so let's load it by running the following command:

```
library(ggplot2)
```

How to do it...

First, let's group points by symbol type. Once again we use the `qplot()` function:

```
qplot(disp,mpg,data=mtcars,shape=as.factor(cyl))
```

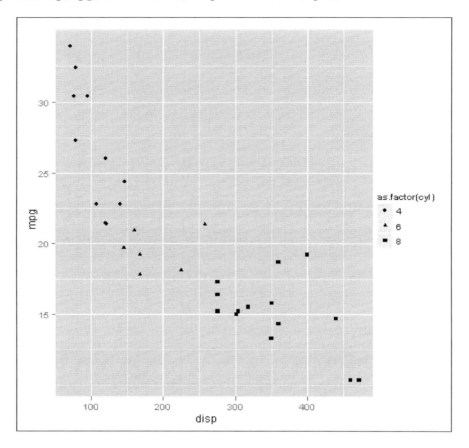

Next, let's group the points simply by the size of the plotting symbol:

```
qplot(disp,mpg,data=mtcars,size=as.factor(cyl))
```

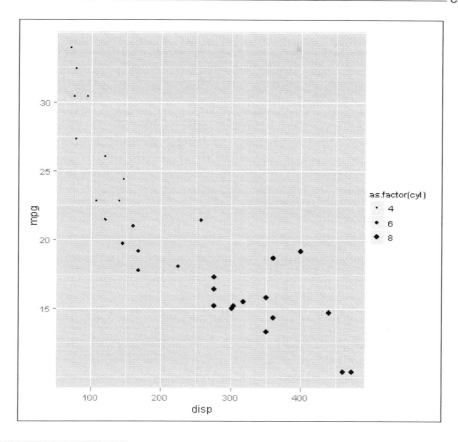

How it works...

Highlighting groups of points by symbol type and size works exactly like color using the `qplot()` functions. Instead of the `col` argument, we used the `shape` and `size` arguments and set them to the factor we want to group the points by (in this case `cyl`). We can also use combinations of any of these arguments. For example, we could use color to represent `cyl` and size to represent gear.

Labelling data points

In this recipe, we will learn how to label individual or multiple data points with text.

Getting ready

For this recipe, we don't need to load any additional libraries. We just need to type the recipe at the R prompt or run it as a script.

How to do it...

Let's say we want to highlight one data point in the cars scatter plot we used in the last few recipes. We can label it using the `text()` command:

```
plot(mpg~disp, data=mtcars)
text(258,22,"Hornet")
```

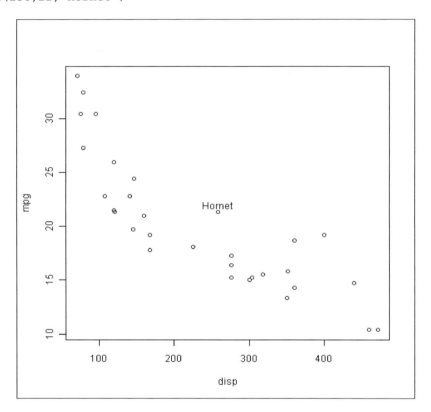

How it works...

In the previous example, we first plotted the graph and then used the `text()` function to overlay a label at a specific location. The `text()` function takes the x and y co-ordinates and text of the label as arguments. We specified the location as `(258,22)` and the label text as `Hornet`. This function is especially useful when we want to label outliers.

There's more...

We can also use the `text()` function to label all the data points in a graph, instead of just one or two. Let's look at another example where we wish to plot the life expectancy in countries versus their health expenditure. Instead of representing the data as points, let's use the name of countries to represent the values. We will use the example dataset `HealthExpenditure.csv`:

```
health<-read.csv("HealthExpenditure.csv",header=TRUE)
plot(health$Expenditure,health$Life_Expectancy,type="n")
text(health$Expenditure,health$Life_Expectancy,health$Country)
```

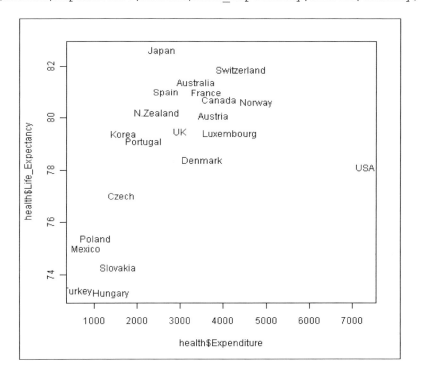

We first use `plot()` command to make a graph of life expectancy versus expenditure. Note that we set `type` equal to `"n"`, which means that only the graph layout and axes are drawn but no data points are drawn. Then we use the `text()` function to place country names as labels at the x-y locations of all the data points. Thus, `text()` accepts vectors as values for (x, y) and labels to dynamically label all the data points with the corresponding country names. In case the text labels overlap, we can use the `jitter()` function or remove some labels to reduce the overlap.

Correlation matrix using pairs plot

In this recipe, we will learn how to create a correlation matrix, which is a handy way of quickly finding out which variables in a dataset are correlated with each other.

Getting ready

To try out this recipe, simply type it at the command prompt. You can also choose to save the recipe as a script so that you can use it again later on.

How to do it...

We will use the iris flowers dataset that we first used in the pairs plot recipe in *Chapter 1*:

```
panel.cor <- function(x, y, ...)
{
    par(usr = c(0, 1, 0, 1))
    txt <- as.character(format(cor(x, y), digits=2))
    text(0.5, 0.5, txt,  cex = 6* abs(cor(x, y)))
}

pairs(iris[1:4], upper.panel=panel.cor)
```

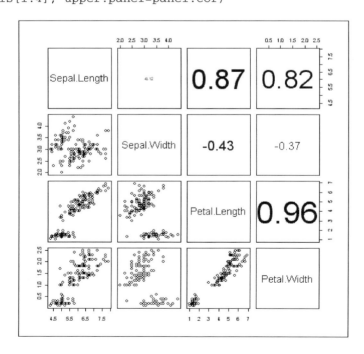

How it works...

We have basically used the `pairs()` function to make the graph, but in addition to the dataset we also set the `upper.panel` argument to `panel.cor`, which is a function we define beforehand. The `upper.panel` argument refers to the squares in the top-right half of the previous graph the diagonal going from the top-left to the bottom-right. Correspondingly, there is also a `lower.panel` argument for the bottom-left half of the graph.

The `panel.cor` value is defined as a function using the following notation:

```
newfunction<-function(arg1, arg2, ...)
{
#function code here
}
```

The `panel.cor` function does a few different things. First it sets the individual panel block axes limits to `c(0,1,0,1)` using the `par()` command. Then it calculates the correlation co-efficient value between a pair of variables up to two decimal values and formats it as a text string so that it can then be passed to the `text()` function which places it in the center of each block. Also note that the size of the labels is set using the `cex` argument to a multiple of the absolute value of the correlation co-efficient. Thus the size of the value label also indicates how important the correlation is.

Panel functions are in fact one of the most powerful features of the lattice package. To learn more about them and the package, please refer to the excellent book *"Lattice: Multivariate Data Visualization with R"* by *Deepayan Sarkar*, who is also the author of the package. The book website is at:
`http://lmdvr.r-forge.r-project.org/figures/figures.html`

Adding error bars

In most scientific data visualization, error bars are necessary to show the level of confidence in the data. However, there is no pre-defined function in the base R library for drawing error bars. In this recipe we will learn how to draw error bars in scatterplots.

Getting ready

All you need for the next recipe is to type it at the R prompt as we will use some base library functions to define a new error bar function. You may also save the recipe code as a script so that you can use it again later on.

How to do it...

Let's draw vertical error bars with 5% errors on our cars scatterplot using the `arrows()` function:

```
plot(mpg~disp,data=mtcars)

arrows(x0=mtcars$disp,
y0=mtcars$mpg*0.95,
x1=mtcars$disp,
y1=mtcars$mpg*1.05,
angle=90,
code=3,
length=0.04,
lwd=0.4)
```

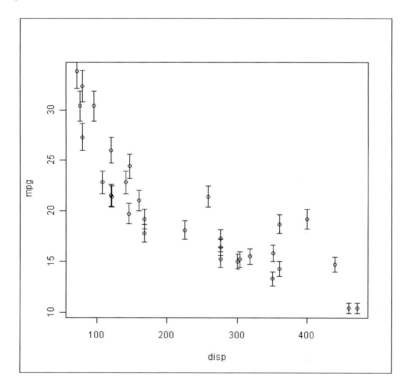

To add horizontal error bars (also 5% in both directions) to the same graph, run the following code after making the earlier graph:

```
arrows(x0=mtcars$disp*0.95,
y0=mtcars$mpg,
```

```
x1=mtcars$disp*1.05,
y1=mtcars$mpg,
angle=90,
code=3,
length=0.04,
lwd=0.4)
```

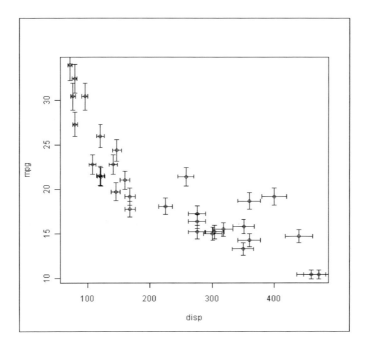

How it works...

In the previous two examples we used the arrows() function to draw horizontal and vertical error bars. arrows() is a base graphics function for drawing different kinds of arrows. It provides various arguments to adjust the size, location, and shape of the arrows such that they can be used as error bars.

The first four arguments define the location of the start and end points of the arrows. The first two arguments x0 and y0 are co-ordinates of the starting points and the next two arguments x1 and y1 are co-ordinates of the end points of the arrows.

For drawing vertical error bars, say with a 5% error both ways, we set both x0 and x1 to the x location of the data points (in this case mtcars$disp) and we set y0 and y1 to the y values of the data points plus and minus the error margin (1.05*mtcars$mpg and 0.95*mtcars$mpg respectively).

Similarly, for drawing horizontal error bars we have the same y co-ordinate for the start and end, but add and subtract the error margin from the x co-ordinates of the data points.

The `angle` argument is for setting the angle between the shaft of the arrow and the edge of the arrowhead. The default value is 30 (which looks more like an arrow), but to use as an error bar we set it to 90 (to flatten out the arrowhead in a way).

The `code` argument sets the type of arrow to be drawn. Setting it to 3 means drawing an arrowhead at both ends.

The `length` and `lwd` arguments set the length of the arrowheads and the line width of the arrow respectively.

There's more...

The `Hmisc` package has the `errbar` function, which can be used to draw vertical error bars. The `plotrix` package has the `plotCI` function which can be used to draw error bars or confidence intervals. If we do not wish to write our own error bars function using `arrows()`, it's easier to use one of these packages.

Using jitter to distinguish closely packed data points

Sometimes when working with large datasets, we may find that a lot of data points on a scatter plot overlap each other. In this recipe we will learn how to distinguish between closely packed data points by adding a small amount of noise with the `jitter()` function.

Getting ready

All you need for the next recipe is to type it at the R prompt as we will use some base library functions to define a new error bar function. You may also save the recipe code as a script so that you can use it again later on.

How to do it...

First let's make a graph which has a lot of overlapping points:

```
x <- rbinom(1000, 10, 0.25)
y <- rbinom(1000, 10, 0.25)
plot(x,y)
```

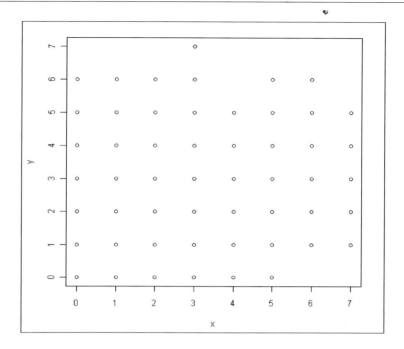

Now, let's add some noise to the data points to see whether there are overlapping points:

```
plot(jitter(x), jitter(y))
```

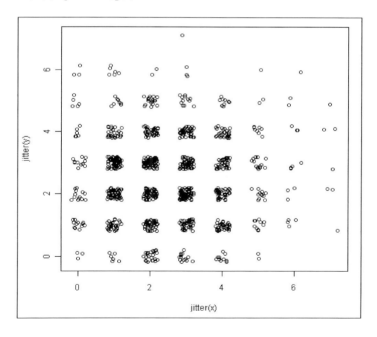

How it works...

In the first graph, we plotted a 1,000 random data points generated with the `rbinom()` function. However, as you can see in the first graph, only a few data points are visible because there are multiple data points in the exact same location. Then when we plotted the points by applying the `jitter()` function to the `x` and `y` values we can see a lot more of the 1,000 points. We can also see that most of the data is in the range of x and y values of 2 to 4.

Adding linear model lines

In this recipe we will learn how to fit a linear model and plot the linear regression line on a scatter plot.

Getting ready

All you need for the next recipe is to type it at the R prompt as we will only use some base functions. You may also save the recipe code as a script so that you can use it again later on.

How to do it...

Once again, let's use the `mtcars` dataset and draw a linear fit line for `mpg` versus `disp`:

```
plot(mtcars$mpg~mtcars$disp)
lmfit<-lm(mtcars$mpg~mtcars$disp)
abline(lmfit)
```

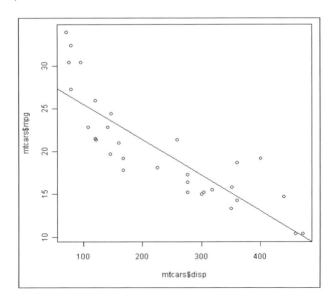

How it works...

We first draw the basic scatter plot of mpg versus disp. Then we fit a linear model to the data using the lm() function, which takes a formula in the form y~x as its argument. Finally, we pass the linear fit to the abline() function, which reads the intercept and slope saved in the lmfit object to draw a line.

Adding non-linear model curves

In this recipe, we will see how to fit and draw a non-linear model curve to a dataset.

Getting ready

All you need for the next recipe is to type it at the R prompt as we will only use some base functions. You may also save the recipe code as a script so that you can use it again later on.

How to do it...

Firstly plot an exponential plot:

```
x <- -(1:100)/10
y <- 100 + 10 * exp(x / 2) + rnorm(x)/10
nlmod <- nls(y ~  Const + A * exp(B * x), trace=TRUE)

plot(x,y)
lines(x, predict(nlmod), col="red")
```

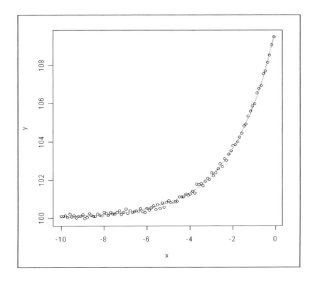

How it works...

We first plot y against x, where x is a variable defined using the sequence operator : and y is an exponential function of x. Then we fit a non-linear model to the data using the `nls()` function. We save the model fit as `nlmod` and finally draw the model predicted values by passing x and `predict(nlmod)` to the `lines()` function.

Adding non-parametric model curves with lowess

In this recipe, we will learn how to use lowess, a non-parametric model, and add the resulting prediction curve to a scatter plot.

Getting ready

For this recipe, we don't need to load any additional libraries. We just need to type the recipe at the R prompt or run it as a script.

How to do it...

First, let's make a simple scatter plot with the pre-loaded cars dataset and add a couple of lowess lines to it:

```
plot(cars, main = "lowess(cars)")
lines(lowess(cars), col = "blue")
lines(lowess(cars, f=0.3), col = "orange")
```

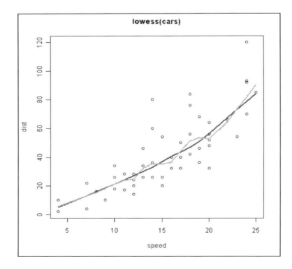

How it works...

Standard R sessions include the `lowess()` function. It is a smoother which uses locally weighted polynomial regression. The first argument, in this instance, is a data frame called `cars` giving the `x` and `y` variables (**speed** and **dist**). So we apply the `lowess` function to the dataset `cars` and in turn pass that result to the `lines()` function. The result of `lowess` is a list with components named x and y. The `lines()` function automatically detects that and uses the appropriate values to draw a smooth line through the scatter plot. The second smooth line has an additional argument `f`, which is known as the smoother span. This gives the proportion of points in the plot which influence the smoothening at each value. Larger values give more smoothness. The default value is approximately 0.67, so when we changed it to 0.3 we get a less smooth fit.

Making three-dimensional scatter plots

In this recipe we will learn how to make three-dimensional scatter plots which can be very useful when we want to explore the relationships between more than two variables at a time.

Getting ready

We need to install and load the `scatterplot3d` package in order to run this recipe:

```
install.packages("scatterplot3d")
library(scatterplot3d)
```

How to do it...

Let's make the simplest default 3D-scatter plot with our `mtcars` dataset:

```
scatterplot3d(x=mtcars$wt,
              y=mtcars$disp,
              z=mtcars$mpg)
```

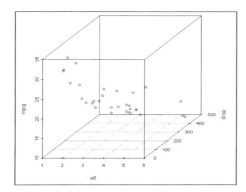

How it works...

That was easy! The `scatterplot3d()` functions much like the basic `plot()` function. In the previous example all we had to provide were `wt`, `disp`, and `mpg` from the `mtcars` dataset as the `x`, `y`, and `z` arguments respectively.

There's more...

Just like `plot()` and other graph functions, `scatterplot3d()` accepts a number of additional arguments using which we can configure the graph in many ways. Let's try some of these additional settings.

Let's add a title to the graph, change the plotting symbol and the angle of viewing, add highlighting, and add vertical drop lines to the x-y plane:

```
scatterplot3d(mtcars$wt,mtcars$disp,mtcars$mpg,
pch=16, highlight.3d=TRUE, angle=20,
xlab="Weight",ylab="Displacement",zlab="Fuel Economy (mpg)",
type="h",
main="Relationships between car specifications")
```

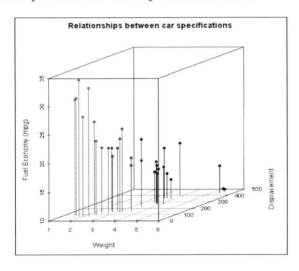

As you can see, we changed some of the graph settings using arguments we have already used before in the `plot()` function. These include the axis titles, graph title, and symbol type. In addition, we added some color highlighting by setting the `highlight.3d` argument to `TRUE`, which draws the points in different colors related to the y co-ordinates (`disp`). The `angle` argument is used to set the angle between the x and y axes, which controls the point from which we view the data. Finally, setting `type` to `h` adds the vertical lines to the x-y plane, which makes reading the graph easier.

For more advanced three-dimensional data visualization in R, please have a look at the `rggobi` package, which allows interactive analysis with 3D plots. The package can be installed like any other R package:

```
install.packages("rggobi")
```

Please see the package website for more details at http://www.ggobi.org/rggobi/.

How to make Quantile-Quantile plots

In this recipe, we will see how to make Quantile-Quantile (Q-Q) plots, which are useful for comparing two probability distributions.

Getting ready

For this recipe, we don't need to load any additional libraries. We just need to type the recipe at the R prompt or run it as a script.

How to do it...

Let's see how the distribution of mpg in the mtcars dataset compares with a normal distribution using the qnorm() function:

```
qqnorm(mtcars$mpg)
qqline(mtcars$mpg)
```

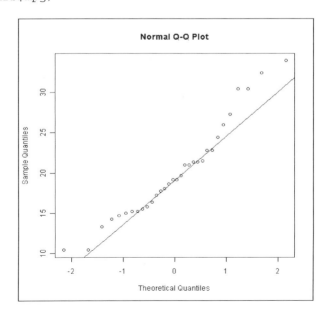

How it works...

In the example, we used the `qqnorm()` function to create a normal Q-Q plot of `mpg` values. We added a straight line with the `qqline()` function. The closer the dots to this line the closer the distribution to a normal one.

There's more...

Another way of making a Q-Q plot is by calling the `plot()` function on a model fit. For example, let's plot the following linear model fit:

```
lmfit<-lm(mtcars$mpg~mtcars$disp)
par(mfrow=c(2,2))
plot(lmfit)
```

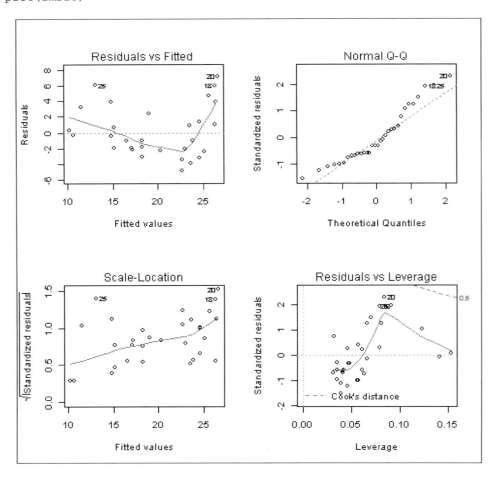

The second plot is a Q-Q plot comparing the model fit to a normal distribution.

Displaying data density on axes

In this recipe, we will learn to show the density of data points on a scatter plot in the margin of the X or Y axes.

Getting ready

For this recipe, we don't need to load any additional libraries.

How to do it...

We will use the rug() function in the base graphics library. As a simple example to illustrate the use of this function, let's see the data density of a normal distribution:

```
x<-rnorm(1000)
plot(density(x))
rug(x)
```

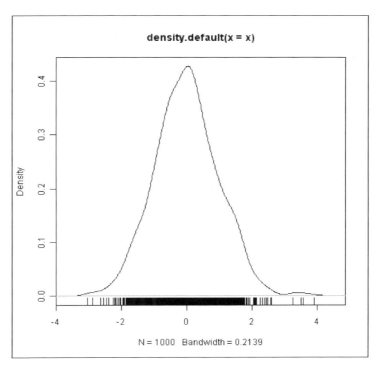

How it works...

As can be seen from the example, the `rug()` function adds a set of lines just above the X axis. A line or tick mark is placed wherever there is a point at that particular X location. So, the more closely packed together the lines are, the higher the data density around those X values is. The example is obvious as we know that in a normal distribution most values are around the mean value (in this case zero).

The `rug()` function in its simplest form only takes one numeric vector as its argument. Note that it draws on top of an existing plot.

There's more...

Let's take another example and explore some of the additional arguments that can be passed to `rug()`. We will use the example `metals.csv` dataset:

```
metals<-read.csv("metals.csv")
plot(Ba~Cu,data=metals,xlim=c(0,100))
rug(metals$Cu)
rug(metals$Ba,side=2,col="red",ticksize=0.02)
```

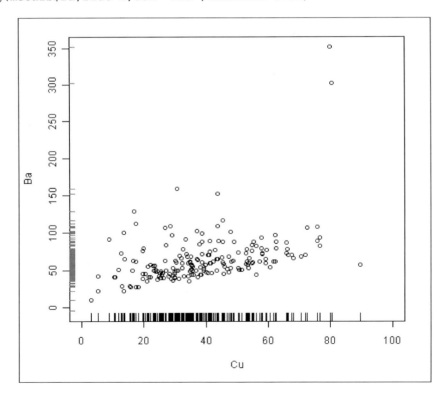

We first read the `metals.csv` file and plot barium (Ba) concentrations against copper (Cu) concentrations. Next, we added a `rug` of Cu values on the X axis using the default settings. Then we added another `rug` for Ba values on the Y axis by setting the `side` argument to 2. The `side` argument takes four values:

- ▶ 1: bottom axis (default)
- ▶ 2: left
- ▶ 3: top
- ▶ 4: right

We also set the color of the tick marks to red using the `col` argument. Finally, we adjusted the size of the tick marks using the `ticksize` argument which reads numeric values as a fraction of the width of the plotting area. Positive values draw inward ticks and negative values draw ticks on the outside.

Making scatter plots with smoothed density representation

Smoothed density scatter plots are a good way of visualizing large datasets. In this recipe, we will learn how to make them using the `smoothScatter()` function.

Getting ready

For this recipe, we don't need to load any additional libraries. We just need to type the recipe at the R prompt or run it as a script.

How to do it...

We will use the `smoothScatter()` function which is part of the base graphics library. We will use an example from the help file which can be accessed from the R prompt with the help command:

```
n <- 10000
x   <- matrix(rnorm(n), ncol=2)
y   <- matrix(rnorm(n, mean=3, sd=1.5), ncol=2)
smoothScatter(x,y)
```

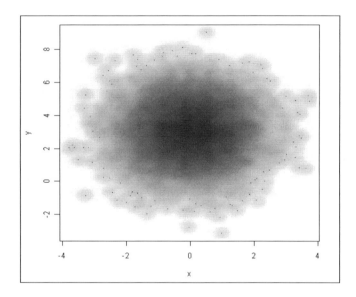

How it works...

The `smoothScatter()` function produces a smoothed color density representation of the scatter plot, obtained through a kernel density estimate. We passed the x and y variables which represented the data to be plotted. The gradient of the blue color shows the density of the data points, with most points in the center of the graph. The dots in the outer light blue circles are outliers.

There's more...

We can pass a number of arguments to `smoothScatter()` to adjust the smoothing, for example `nbin` for specifying the number of equally spaced grid points for the density estimation, and `nrpoints` to specify how many points to show as dots. In addition, we can also pass standard arguments such as `xlab`, `ylab`, `pch`, `cex`, and so on to modify axis and plotting symbol characteristics.

4

Creating Line Graphs and Time Series Charts

In this chapter, we will cover:

- ▶ Adding customized legends for multiple line graphs
- ▶ Using margin labels instead of legends for multiple line graphs
- ▶ Adding horizontal and vertical grid lines
- ▶ Adding marker lines at specific X and Y values
- ▶ Creating sparklines
- ▶ Plotting functions of a variable in a dataset
- ▶ Formatting time series data for plotting
- ▶ Plotting date and time on the X axis
- ▶ Annotating axis labels in different human readable time formats
- ▶ Adding vertical markers to indicate specific time events
- ▶ Plotting data with varying time averaging periods
- ▶ Creating stock charts

Introduction

In *Chapter 1, Basic Graph Functions* and *Chapter 2, Beyond the Basics: Adjusting Key Parameters*, we learnt some basics of how to make line graphs and customize them by setting certain arguments as per our needs. In this chapter, we will learn some more intermediate to advanced recipes for customizing line graphs even further. We will look at ways to improve and speed up line graphs with multiple lines representing more than one variable.

One of the most used form of line graphs is time trends or time series, where the X variable is some measure of time such as year, month, week, day, hour, and so on. Reading, formatting, and plotting dates can be quite tricky in R. In this chapter, we will see how to deal with dates and process them to make time series charts with custom annotations, grid lines, uncertainty bounds, and markers.

We will also learn to make some interesting and popular types of time series charts such as sparklines and stock charts.

As the recipes in this chapter are slightly more advanced than the earlier chapters, it may take some practice with multiple datasets before you are comfortable with using all the functions. Example datasets are used in each recipe, but it is highly recommended to also work with your own datasets and modify the recipes to suit your own analysis.

Adding customized legends for multiple line graphs

Line graphs with more than one line, representing more than one variable, are quite common in any kind of data analysis. In this recipe we will learn how to create and customize legends for such graphs.

Getting ready

We will use the base graphics library for this recipe, so all you need to do is run the recipe at the R prompt. It is good practice to save your code as a script to use again later.

How to do it...

Once again we will use the `cityrain.csv` example dataset that we used in *Chapter 1* and *Chapter 2*.

```
rain<-read.csv("cityrain.csv")
plot(rain$Tokyo,type="b",lwd=2,
xaxt="n",ylim=c(0,300),col="black",
xlab="Month",ylab="Rainfall (mm)",
```

```
main="Monthly Rainfall in major cities")
axis(1,at=1:length(rain$Month),labels=rain$Month)
lines(rain$Berlin,col="red",type="b",lwd=2)
lines(rain$NewYork,col="orange",type="b",lwd=2)
lines(rain$London,col="purple",type="b",lwd=2)

legend("topright",legend=c("Tokyo","Berlin","New York","London"),
lty=1,lwd=2,pch=21,col=c("black","red","orange","purple"),
ncol=2,bty="n",cex=0.8,
text.col=c("black","red","orange","purple"),
inset=0.01)
```

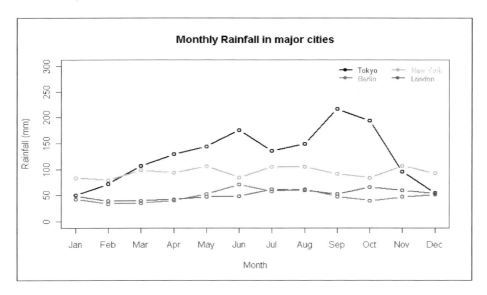

How it works...

We used the legend() function, which we have already come across in earlier chapters. It is quite a flexible function and allows us to adjust the placement and styling of the legend in many ways.

The first argument we passed to legend() specifies the position of the legend within the plot region. We used "topright"; other possible values are "bottomright", "bottom", "bottomleft", "left", "topleft", "top", "right", and "center". We can also specify the location of legend with x and y co-ordinates as we will soon see.

The other important arguments specific to lines are `lwd` and `lty` which specify the line width and type drawn in the legend box respectively. It is important to keep these the same as the corresponding values in the `plot()` and `lines()` commands. We also set `pch` to 21 to replicate the `type="b"` argument in the `plot()` command. `cex` and `text.col` set the size and colors of the legend text. Note that we set the text colors to the same colors as the lines they represent. Setting `bty` (box type) to `"n"` ensures no box is drawn around the legend. This is good practice as it keeps the look of the graph clean. `ncol` sets the number of columns over which the legend labels are spread and `inset` sets the inset distance from the margins as a fraction of the plot region.

There's more...

Let's experiment by changing some of the arguments discussed:

```
legend(1,300,legend=c("Tokyo","Berlin","New York","London"),
lty=1,lwd=2,pch=21,col=c("black","red","orange","purple"),
horiz=TRUE,bty="n",bg="yellow",cex=1,
text.col=c("black","red","orange","purple"))
```

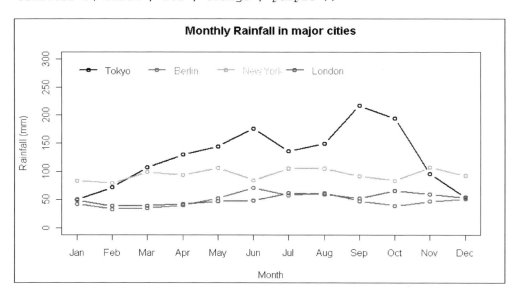

This time we used x and y co-ordinates instead of a keyword to position the legend. We also set the `horiz` argument to `TRUE`. As the name suggests, `horiz` makes the legend labels horizontal instead of the default vertical. Specifying `horiz` overrides the `ncol` argument. Finally, we made the legend text bigger by setting `cex` to 1 and did not use the `inset` argument.

An alternative way of creating the previous plot without having to call `plot()` and `lines()` multiple times is to use the `matplot()` function. To see details on how to use this function, please see the help file by running `?matplot` or `help(matplot)` at the R prompt.

See also

Have a look at the next recipe, which shows a way to label lines directly instead of using a legend.

Using margin labels instead of legends for multiple line graphs

While legends are the most commonly used method of providing a key to read multiple variable graphs, they are often not the easiest to read. Labelling lines directly is one way of getting around that problem.

Getting ready

We will use the base graphics library for this recipe, so all you need to do is run the recipe at the R prompt. It is good practice to save your code as a script to use again later.

How to do it...

Let's use the `gdp.txt` example dataset to look at the trends in the annual GDP of five countries:

```
gdp<-read.table("gdp_long.txt",header=T)

library(RColorBrewer)
pal<-brewer.pal(5,"Set1")

par(mar=par()$mar+c(0,0,0,2),bty="l")

plot(Canada~Year,data=gdp,type="l",lwd=2,lty=1,ylim=c(30,60),
col=pal[1],main="Percentage change in GDP",ylab="")

mtext(side=4,at=gdp$Canada[length(gdp$Canada)],text="Canada",
col=pal[1],line=0.3,las=2)

lines(gdp$France~gdp$Year,col=pal[2],lwd=2)

mtext(side=4,at=gdp$France[length(gdp$France)],text="France",
```

```
col=pal[2],line=0.3,las=2)

lines(gdp$Germany~gdp$Year,col=pal[3],lwd=2)

mtext(side=4,at=gdp$Germany[length(gdp$Germany)],text="Germany",
col=pal[3],line=0.3,las=2)

lines(gdp$Britain~gdp$Year,col=pal[4],lwd=2)

mtext(side=4,at=gdp$Britain[length(gdp$Britain)],text="Britain",
col=pal[4],line=0.3,las=2)

lines(gdp$USA~gdp$Year,col=pal[5],lwd=2)

mtext(side=4,at=gdp$USA[length(gdp$USA)]-2,
text="USA",col=pal[5],line=0.3,las=2)
```

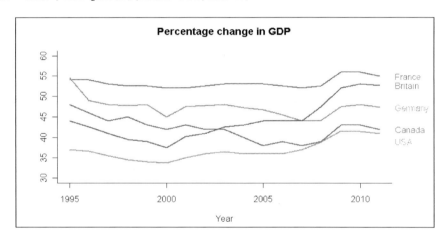

How it works...

We first read the gdp.txt data file using the read.table() function. Next we loaded the RColorBrewer color palette library and set our color palette pal to "Set1" (with five colors).

Before drawing the graph, we used the par() command to add extra space to the right margin, so that we have enough space for the labels. Depending on the size of the text labels you may have to experiment with this margin until you get it right. Finally, we set the box type (bty) to an L-shape ("l") so that there is no line on the right margin. We can also set it to "c" if we want to keep the top line.

We used the `mtext()` function to label each of the lines individually in the right margin. The first argument we passed to the function is the side where we want the label to be placed. Sides (margins) are numbered starting from 1 for the bottom side and going round in a clockwise direction so that 2 is left, 3 is top, and 4 is right.

The `at` argument was used to specify the Y co-ordinate of the label. This is a bit tricky because we have to make sure we place the label as close to the corresponding line as possible. So, here we have used the last value of each line. For example, `gdp$France[length(gdp$France)]` picks the last value in the France vector by using its length as the index. Note that we had to adjust the value for USA by subtracting 2 from its last value so that it doesn't overlap the label for Canada.

We used the `text` argument to set the text of the labels as country names. We set the `col` argument to the appropriate element of the `pal` vector by using a number index. The `line` argument sets an offset in terms of margin lines, starting at 0 counting outwards. Finally, setting `las` to 2 rotates the labels to be perpendicular to the axis, instead of the default value of 1 which makes them parallel to the axis.

There's more...

Sometimes, simply using the last value of a set of values may not work because the value may be missing. In that case we can use the second last value or visually choose a value that places the label closest to the line. Also, the size of the plot window and the proximity of the final values may cause overlapping of labels. So, we may need to iterate a few times before we get the placement right. We can write functions to automate this process but it is still good to visually inspect the outcome.

Adding horizontal and vertical grid lines

In this recipe we will learn how to add and customize grid lines to graphs.

Getting ready

We will use the base graphics for this recipe, so all you need to do is run the recipe at the R prompt. It is good practice to save your code as a script to use again later.

How to do it...

Let's use the city rainfall example again to see how we can add grid lines to that graph:

```
rain<-read.csv("cityrain.csv")
plot(rain$Tokyo,type="b",lwd=2,
xaxt="n",ylim=c(0,300),col="black",
xlab="Month",ylab="Rainfall (mm)",
main="Monthly Rainfall in Tokyo")
axis(1,at=1:length(rain$Month),labels=rain$Month)

grid()
```

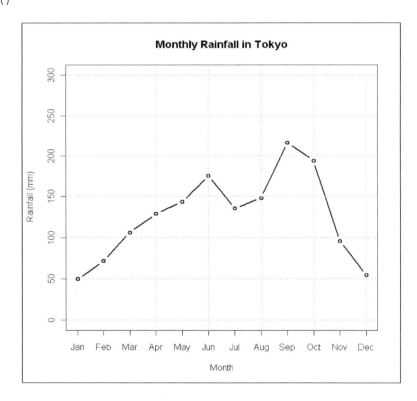

How it works...

It's as simple as that! Adding a simple default grid just needs calling the `grid()` function without passing any arguments. `grid()` automatically computes the number of cells in the grid and aligns with the tick marks on the default axes. It uses the `abline()` function (which we will see again in the next recipe) to draw the grid lines.

There's more...

We can specify the location of the grid lines using the nx and ny arguments, corresponding to vertical and horizontal grid lines respectively. By default, these two arguments are set to NULL, which results in the default grid lines in both X and Y directions. If we do not wish to draw grid lines in a particular direction, we can set nx or ny to NA. If nx is set to NA, no vertical grid lines are drawn and if ny is set to NA, no horizontal grid lines are drawn.

The default grid lines are very thin and light colored, they can barely be seen. We can customize the styling of the grid lines using the lwd, lty, and col arguments.

```
grid(nx=NA, ny=8,
lwd=1,lty=2,col="blue")
```

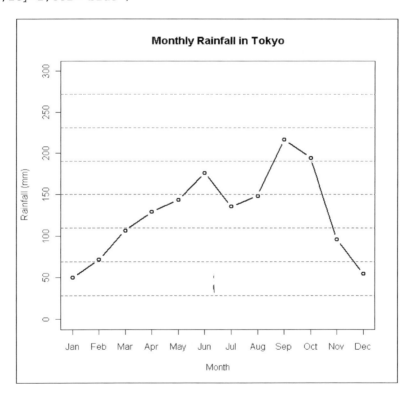

See also

In the next recipe we will learn to use the abline() function, which we can use to draw lines at any specific X and Y locations.

Adding marker lines at specific X and Y values

Sometimes we may only want to draw one or a few lines to indicate specific cut-off or threshold values. In this recipe, we will learn how to do that using the `abline()` function.

Getting ready

We will use the base graphics library for this recipe, so all you need to do is run the recipe at the R prompt. It is good practice to save your code as a script to use again later.

How to do it...

Let's draw a vertical line at the month of September in the rainfall graph for Tokyo:

```
rain <- read.csv("cityrain.csv")
plot(rain$Tokyo,type="b",lwd=2,
xaxt="n",ylim=c(0,300),col="black",
xlab="Month",ylab="Rainfall (mm)",
main="Monthly Rainfall in Tokyo")
axis(1,at=1:length(rain$Month),labels=rain$Month)

abline(v=9)
```

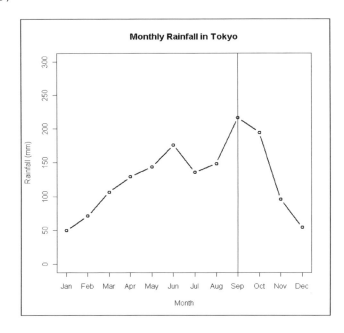

How it works...

To draw marker lines with `abline()` at specific X or Y locations, we have to set the v (as in vertical) or h (as in horizontal) arguments respectively. In the example, we set v=9 (the index of the month September in the Month vector).

There's more...

Now let's add a red dotted horizontal line to the graph to denote a high rainfall cutoff of 150 mm:

```
abline(h=150,col="red",lty=2)
```

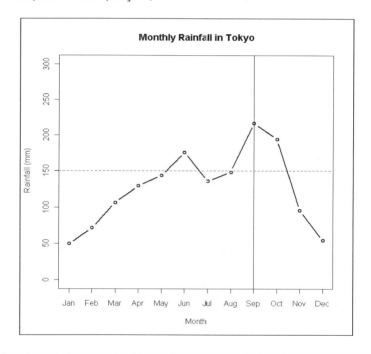

Creating sparklines

Sparklines are small and simple line graphs, useful for summarizing trend data in a small space. The word "sparklines" was coined by Prof. Edward Tufte. In this recipe we will learn how to make sparklines using a basic `plot()` function.

Getting ready

We will use the base graphics library for this recipe, so all you need to do is run the recipe at the R prompt. It is good practice to save your code as a script to use again later.

How to do it...

Let's represent our city rainfall data in the form of sparklines:

```
rain <- read.csv("cityrain.csv")

par(mfrow=c(4,1),mar=c(5,7,4,2),omi=c(0.2,2,0.2,2))

for(i in 2:5)
{
    plot(rain[,i],ann=FALSE,axes=FALSE,type="l",
    col="gray",lwd=2)

    mtext(side=2,at=mean(rain[,i]),names(rain[i]),
    las=2,col="black")

    mtext(side=4,at=mean(rain[,i]),mean(rain[i]),
    las=2,col="black")

    points(which.min(rain[,i]),min(rain[,i]),pch=19,col="blue")
    points(which.max(rain[,i]),max(rain[,i]),pch=19,col="red")
}
```

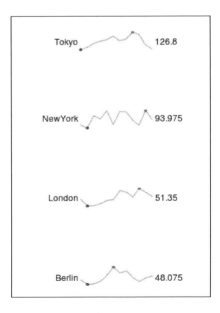

How it works...

The key feature of sparklines is to show the trend in the data with just one line without any axis annotations. In the example, we have shown the trend with a gray line. The minimum and maximum values for each line is represented by blue and red dots respectively, while the mean value is displayed on the right margin.

Since sparklines have to be very small graphics, we first set the margins such that the plot area is small and the outer margins are large. We did this by setting the outer margins in inches using the `omi` argument of the `par()` function. Depending on the dimensions of the plot, sometimes R may produce an error saying that the figure margins are too large and not draw the graph. In that case, we need to try lower values for the margins. Note we also set up a 4x1 layout with the `mfrow` argument.

Next we set up a `for` loop to draw a sparkline for each of the four cities. We drew the line with the `plot()` command, setting both annotations (ann) and axes to `false`. Then we used the `mtext()` function to place the name of the city and the mean value of rainfall to the left and right of the line respectively. Finally, we plotted the minimum and maximum values using the `points()` command. Note we use the `which.min()` and `which.max()` functions to get the indices of the minimum and maximum values respectively and used them as the x value for the `points()` function calls.

Plotting functions of a variable in a dataset

Sometimes we may wish to visualize the effect of applying a mathematical function to a set of values, instead of the original variable itself. In this recipe, we will see a simple method to plot functions of variables.

Getting ready

We will use the base graphics library for this recipe, so all you need to do is run the recipe at the R prompt. It is good practice to save your code as a script to use again later.

How to do it...

Let's say we want to plot the difference in rainfall between Tokyo and London. We can do that just by passing the correct expression to the `plot()` function:

```
rain <- read.csv("cityrain.csv")

plot(rain$Berlin-rain$London,type="l",lwd=2,
xaxt="n",col="blue",
xlab="Month",ylab="Difference in Rainfall (mm)",
main="Difference in Rainfall between Berlin and London (Berlin-
```

```
London)")

axis(1,at=1:length(rain$Month),labels=rain$Month)

abline(h=0,col="red")
```

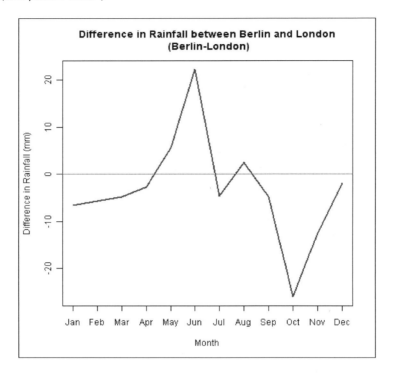

How it works...

So, plotting a function of a variable is as simple as passing an expression to the `plot()` function. In the example, the function consisted of two variables in the dataset. We can also plot transformations applied to any one variable.

There's more...

As another simple example, let's see how we can plot a polynomial function of a set of numbers:

```
x<-1:100
y<-x^3-6*x^2+5*x+10
plot(y~x,type="l",main=expression(f(x)==x^3-6*x^2+5*x+10))
```

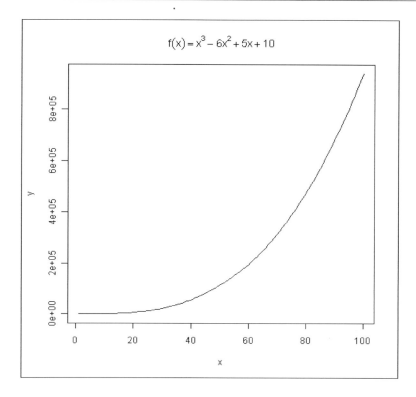

In this example we defined y as a polynomial function of a vector of the numbers 1 to 100 and then plotted it using the plot() function. Note that we used the expression() function to format the title of the graph. By using expression() we could get the power values as superscripts.

Formatting time series data for plotting

Time series or trend charts are the most common form of line graphs. There are a lot of ways in R to plot such data, however it is important to first format the data in a suitable format that R can understand. In this recipe, we will look at some ways of formatting time series data using the base and some additional packages.

Getting ready

In addition to the basic R functions, we will also be using the zoo package in this recipe. So first we need to install it:

```
install.packages("zoo")
```

How to do it...

Let's use the `dailysales.csv` example dataset and format its `date` column:

```
sales<-read.csv("dailysales.csv")

d1<-as.Date(sales$date,"%d/%m/%y")

d2<-strptime(sales$date,"%d/%m/%y")

data.class(d1)
[1] "Date"

data.class(d2)
[1] "POSIXt"
```

How it works...

We have seen two different functions to convert a character vector into dates. If we did not convert the `date` column, R would not automatically recognize the values in the column as dates. Instead, the column would be treated as a character vector or a factor.

The `as.Date()` function takes at least two arguments: the character vector to be converted to dates and the format to which we want it converted. It returns an object of the `Date` class, represented as the number of days since 1970-01-01, with negative values for earlier dates. The values in the `date` column are in a DD/MM/YYYY format (you can verify this by typing `sales$date` at the R prompt). So, we specify the format argument as `"%d/%m/%y"`. Please note that this order is important. If we instead use `"%m/%d/%y"`, then our days will be read as months and vice-versa. The quotes around the value are also necessary.

The `strptime()` function is another way to convert character vectors into dates. However, `strptime()` returns a different kind of object of class `POSIXlt`, which is a named list of vectors representing the different components of a date and time, such as year, month, day, hour, seconds, minutes, and a few more.

POSIXlt is one of the two basic classes of date/times in R. The other class POSIXct represents the (signed) number of seconds since the beginning of 1970 (in the UTC time zone) as a numeric vector. POSIXct is more convenient for including in data frames, and POSIXlt is closer to human readable forms. A virtual class POSIXt inherits from both of the classes. That's why when we ran the data.class() function on d2 earlier, we get POSIXt as the result.

strptime() also takes a character vector to be converted and the format as arguments.

There's more...

The zoo package is handy for dealing with time series data. The zoo() function takes an argument x, which can be a numeric vector, matrix, or factor. It also takes an order.by argument which has to be an index vector with unique entries by which the observations in x are ordered:

```
library(zoo)

d3<-zoo(sales$units,as.Date(sales$date,"%d/%m/%y"))

data.class(d3)
[1] "zoo"
```

See the help on DateTimeClasses to find out more details about the ways dates can be represented in R.

Plotting date and time on the X axis

In this recipe, we will learn how to plot formatted date or time values on the X axis.

Getting ready

For the first example, we only need to use the base graphics function plot().

How to do it...

We will use the `dailysales.csv` example dataset to plot the number of units of a product sold daily in a month:

```
sales<-read.csv("dailysales.csv")
plot(sales$units~as.Date(sales$date,"%d/%m/%y"),type="l",
xlab="Date",ylab="Units Sold")
```

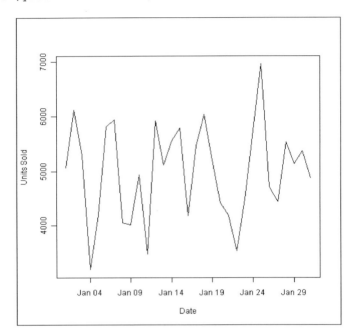

How it works...

Once we have formatted the series of dates using `as.Date()`, we can simply pass it to the `plot()` function as the x variable in either the `plot(x,y)` or `plot(y~x)` format.

We can also use `strptime()` instead of using `as.Date()`. However, we cannot pass the object returned by `strptime()` to `plot()` in the `plot(y~x)` format. We must use the `plot(x,y)` format as follows:

```
plot(strptime(sales$date,"%d/%m/%Y"),sales$units,type="l",
xlab="Date",ylab="Units Sold")
```

There's more...

We can plot the example using the `zoo()` function as follows (assuming zoo is already installed):

```
library(zoo)
plot(zoo(sales$units,as.Date(sales$date,"%d/%m/%y")))
```

Note that we don't need to specify x and y separately when plotting using `zoo`; we can just pass the object returned by `zoo()` to `plot()`. We also need not specify the type as `"l"`.

Let's look at another example which has full date and time values on the X axis, instead of just dates. We will use the `openair.csv` example dataset for this example:

```
air<-read.csv("openair.csv")

plot(air$nox~as.Date(air$date,"%d/%m/%Y %H:%M"),type="l",
xlab="Time", ylab="Concentration (ppb)",
main="Time trend of Oxides of Nitrogen")
```

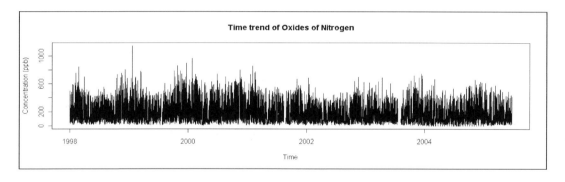

The same graph can be made using zoo as follows:

```
plot(zoo(air$nox,as.Date(air$date,"%d/%m/%Y %H:%M")),
xlab="Time", ylab="Concentration (ppb)",
main="Time trend of Oxides of Nitrogen")
```

Annotating axis labels in different human readable time formats

In this recipe, we will learn how to choose the formatting of time axis labels, instead of just using the defaults.

Getting ready

We will only use the basic R functions for this recipe. Make sure you are at the R prompt and load the `openair.csv` dataset:

```
air<-read.csv("openair.csv")
```

How to do it...

Let's redraw our original example of plotting air pollution data from the last recipe, but with labels for each month and year pairing:

```
plot(air$nox~as.Date(air$date,"%d/%m/%Y %H:%M"),type="l",
xaxt="n",
xlab="Time", ylab="Concentration (ppb)",
main="Time trend of Oxides of Nitrogen")

xlabels<-strptime(air$date, format = "%d/%m/%Y %H:%M")
axis.Date(1, at=xlabels[xlabels$mday==1], format="%b-%Y")
```

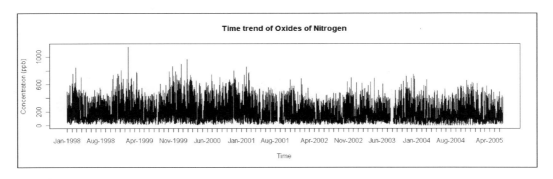

How it works...

In our original example of plotting air pollution data in the last recipe, we only formatted the date/time vector to pass as an x argument to `plot()`, but the axis labels were chosen automatically by R as the years 1998, 2000, 2002, and 2004. In this example, we drew a custom axis with labels for each month and year pairing.

We first created an object `xlabels` of class `POSIXlt` by using the `strptime()` function. Then we used the `axis.Date()` function to add the X axis. `axis.Date()` is similar to the `axis()` function and takes the `side` and `at` arguments. In addition, it also takes the `format` argument, which we can use to specify the format of the labels. We specified the `at` argument as a subset of `xlabels` for only the first day of each month by setting `mday=1`. The format value `"%b-%Y"` means abbreviated month name with full year.

There's more...

See the help on `strptime()` to see all the possible formatting options.

Adding vertical markers to indicate specific time events

We may wish to indicate specific points of importance or measurements in a time series, where there is a significant event or change in the data. In this recipe, we will learn how to add vertical markers using the `abline()` function.

Getting ready

We will only use the basic R functions for this recipe. Make sure you are at the R prompt and load the `openair.csv` dataset:

```
air<-read.csv("openair.csv")
```

How to do it...

Let's take our air pollution time series example again and draw a red vertical line on Christmas day – 25/12/2003:

```
plot(air$nox~as.Date(air$date,"%d/%m/%Y %H:%M"),type="l",
xlab="Time", ylab="Concentration (ppb)",
main="Time trend of Oxides of Nitrogen")

abline(v=as.Date("25/12/2003","%d/%m/%Y"))
```

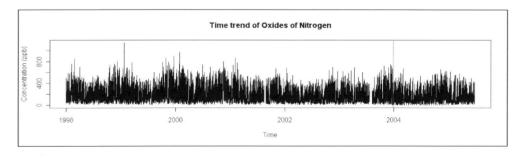

How it works...

As we have seen before in the recipe introducing `abline()`, we drew a vertical line in the example by setting the `v` argument to the date we want to mark. We specified 25/12/2003 as the `x` co-ordinate by using the `as.Date()` function. Note that the original time series plotted also contains the timestamp in addition to the dates. Since we didn't specify a time, the line was plotted at the start of the specified date 25/12/2003 00:00.

There's more...

Let's look at another example, where we want to draw a vertical marker line on Christmas day of every year:

```
markers<-seq(from=as.Date("25/12/1998","%d/%m/%Y"),
to=as.Date("25/12/2004","%d/%m/%Y"),
by="year")

abline(v=markers,col="red")
```

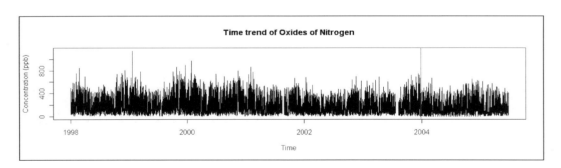

We created a sequence of the Christmas dates for each year using the `seq()` function, which takes `from`, `to`, and `by` arguments. Then we passed this vector to the `abline()` function as `v`.

One important thing to note is that by default R does not deal with gaps in a time series. There can be missing values denoted by `NA` and as you can see in the previous examples, the graphs show gaps in those places. However, if any dates or time intervals are missing from the actual dataset, then R draws a line connecting the data points before and after the gap instead of leaving it blank. In order to remove this connecting line, we must fill in the missing time intervals in the gap and set the `y` values to `NA`.

Plotting data with varying time averaging periods

In this recipe, we will learn how we can plot the same time series data by averaging it over different time periods using the `aggregate()` function.

Getting ready

We will only use the basic R functions for this recipe. Make sure you load the `openair.csv` dataset:

```
air<-read.csv("openair.csv")
```

How to do it...

Let's plot the air pollution time series with weekly and daily averages instead of hourly values:

```
air$date = as.POSIXct(strptime(air$date, format = "%d/%m/%Y %H:%M",
"GMT"))
means <- aggregate(air["nox"], format(air["date"],"%Y-%U"),mean,
na.rm = TRUE)
means$date <- seq(air$date[1], air$date[nrow(air)],
length = nrow(means))
plot(means$date, means$nox, type = "l")
```

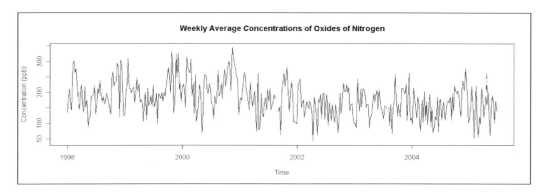

```
means <- aggregate(air["nox"], format(air["date"],"%Y-%j"),mean,
na.rm = TRUE)
means$date <- seq(air$date[1], air$date[nrow(air)],
length = nrow(means))
plot(means$date, means$nox, type = "l",
xlab="Time", ylab="Concentration (ppb)",
main="Daily  Average Concentrations of Oxides of Nitrogen")
```

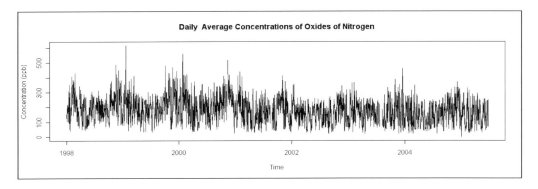

How it works...

The key function in these examples is the `aggregate()` function. Its first argument is R object `x`, which has to be aggregated, in this case `air["nox"]`. The next argument is the list of grouping elements over which `x` has to be aggregated. This is the part where we specify the time period over which to average the values. In the first example we set it to `format(air["date"],"%Y-%U")`, which extracts all the weeks out of the `date` column using the `format()` function. The third argument is `FUN` or the name of the function to apply to the selected values, in our case `mean`. Finally, we set `na.rm` to `TRUE`, thus telling R to ignore missing values denoted by `NA`.

Once we have the mean values saved in a data frame, we add a date field to this new vector using the `seq()` function and then plot the means against the date using `plot()`.

In the second example, we use `format(air["date"],"%Y-%j")` to calculate daily means.

Creating stock charts

Given R's powerful analysis and graphical capabilities, it is no surprise that R is very popular in the world of finance. In this recipe, we will learn how to plot data from the stock market using some special libraries.

Getting ready

We need the `tseries` and `quantmod` packages to run the following recipes. Let's install and load these two packages:

```
install.packages("quantmod")
install.packages("tseries")
library(quantmod)
library(tseries)
```

How to do it...

Let's first see an example using the `tseries` library function `get.hist.quotes()`. We will compare stock prices of three technology companies:

```
aapl<-get.hist.quote(instrument = "aapl", quote = c("Cl", "Vol"))

goog <- get.hist.quote(instrument = "goog", quote = c("Cl", "Vol"))

msft <- get.hist.quote(instrument = "msft", quote = c("Cl", "Vol"))

plot(msft$Close,main = "Stock Price Comparison",
ylim=c(0,800), col="red", type="l", lwd=0.5,
pch=19,cex=0.6, xlab="Date" ,ylab="Stock Price (USD)")

lines(goog$Close,col="blue",lwd=0.5)
lines(aapl$Close,col="gray",lwd=0.5)

legend("top",horiz=T,legend=c("Microsoft","Google","Apple"),
col=c("red","blue","gray"),lty=1,bty="n")
```

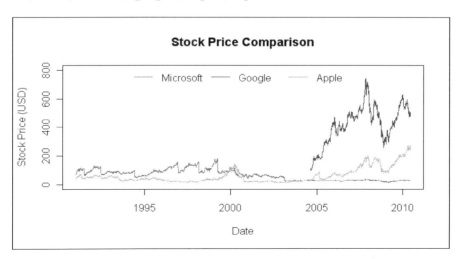

How it works...

The get.hist.quote() function retrieves historical financial data from one of two providers (yahoo (for Yahoo) or oanda (for OANDA), yahoo being the default). We passed the instrument and quote arguments to this function which specify the name of the stock and the measure of stock data we want. In our example, we used the function three times to pull the closing price and volume for Microsoft (msft), Google (goog), and Apple (aapl). We then plotted the three stock prices on a line graph using the plot() and lines() functions.

There's more...

Now let's make some charts using the quantmod package. This package provides inbuilt graphics functions to visualize the stock data:

```
getSymbols("AAPL",src="yahoo")
barChart(AAPL)
```

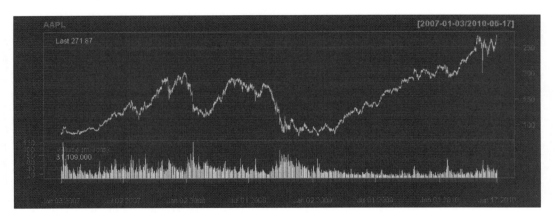

First we obtained stock data for Apple using the getSymbols() function by specifying the stock name and source. Again, the default source is Yahoo. The stock data is stored in an R object with the same name as the stock symbol (AAPL for Apple, GOOG for Google, and so on). Then we passed this object to the barChart() function to produce the previous graph above. Of course, it is more than just a bar chart.

A similar chart in a different color scheme can be drawn as follows:

```
candleChart(AAPL,theme="white")
```

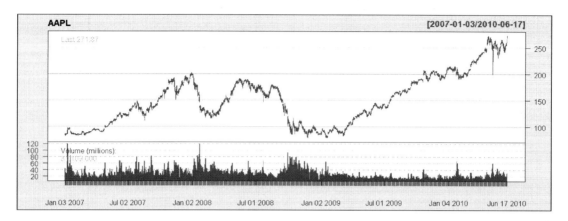

For more detailed information about the `quantmod package`, visit its website at:
`http://www.quantmod.com`

5
Creating Bar, Dot, and Pie Charts

In this chapter, we will cover:

- ▶ Creating bar charts with more than one factor variable
- ▶ Creating stacked bar charts
- ▶ Adjusting the orientation of bars—horizontal and vertical
- ▶ Adjusting bar widths, spacing, colors, and borders
- ▶ Displaying values on top of or next to the bars
- ▶ Placing labels inside bars
- ▶ Creating bar charts with vertical error bars
- ▶ Modifying dot charts by grouping variables
- ▶ Making better readable pie charts with clockwise-ordered slices
- ▶ Labelling a pie chart with percentage values for each slice
- ▶ Adding a legend to a pie chart

Introduction

In this chapter, we will look in some detail at bar charts, dot charts, and pie charts. Bar charts are used commonly both in reporting business data and also in scientific analysis. We will see how we can enhance the basic bar charts in R by adjusting some parameters in the base graphics library. There are a few different packages which can be used to make bar charts (most notably `lattice` and `ggplot2`). But in this chapter, we will see how we can create many useful variations of bar graphs only by using the base library functions.

We will also look at a few recipes on pie charts—easily the most criticized type of chart in the scientific community, but also one of the most popular in the business world. While it is true that pie charts often obscure the data and are hard to read, the recipes in this chapter offer some ways to make pie charts more readable.

Some of the parameters are obscure and sometimes it may not be absolutely clear as to what values an argument can take. It is best to experiment as you go along and try out the recipes. You may not understand a function or its arguments fully, until you have tried to graph a few of your own datasets. If you get stuck at any point, first look at the help file of the relevant function. If you are still stuck after having read the help files, then you may search the R mailing list (`http://www.r-project.org/mail.html`) and forums (`http://r.789695.n4.nabble.com/` and `http://stackoverflow.com/questions/tagged/r`). Often, the problems one comes across are common and may have already been addressed by the R community in response to someone else's question.

Creating bar charts with more than one factor variable

In this first recipe, we will learn how to make bar charts for data with more than one category. Such bar charts are commonly used for comparing values of the same measure across different categories.

Getting ready

We will be using the base library `barplot()` function, but we will also use the `RColorBrewer` package to choose a good color palette. So let's first install and load that package:

```
install.packages("RColorBrewer") #if not already installed
library(RColorBrewer)
```

How to do it...

Let's use the `citysales.csv` example dataset that we used in the first chapter once again:

```
citysales<-read.csv("citysales.csv")

barplot(as.matrix(citysales[,2:4]), beside=TRUE,
legend.text=citysales$City,
args.legend=list(bty="n",horiz=TRUE),
col=brewer.pal(5,"Set1"),
border="white",ylim=c(0,100),
ylab="Sales Revenue (1,000's of USD)",
```

```
main="Sales Figures")

box(bty="l")
```

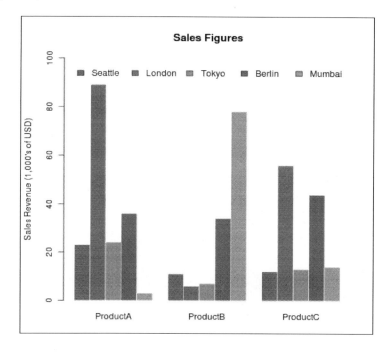

How it works...

The key argument for drawing bar charts with more than one category is the beside argument, which must be set to TRUE. The first argument is the input data, which must be in the form of a matrix. The columns of the matrix are the categories (in this case ProductA, ProductB, and ProductC), while the rows are the set of values for each category. If we do not set the beside argument to TRUE, we will get a stacked bar chart (as we will see later in this chapter).

Most of the other arguments of the barplot() function work the same way as they do for plot(). The args.legend argument takes a list of arguments and passes them on to the legend() function. We can instead also call the legend() function separately after the barplot() call.

See also

In the next recipe, we will learn how to make stacked bar charts.

Creating stacked bar charts

Stacked bar charts are another form of bar charts used to compare values across categories. As the name implies, the bars for each category are stacked on top of each other instead of being placed next to each other.

Getting ready

We will use the same dataset and color scheme as the last recipe, so please ensure you have the `RColorBrewer` package installed and loaded:

```
install.packages("RColorBrewer")
library(RColorBrewer)
```

How to do it...

Let's draw a stacked bar chart of sales figures across the five cities:

```
citysales<-read.csv("citysales.csv")

barplot(as.matrix(citysales[,2:4]),
legend.text=citysales$City,
args.legend=list(bty="n",horiz=TRUE),
col=brewer.pal(5,"Set1"),border="white",
ylim=c(0,200),ylab="Sales Revenue (1,000's of USD)",
main="Sales Figures")
```

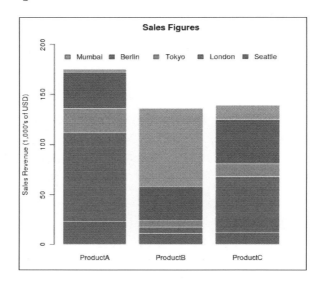

How it works...

If you compare the code for this example and the last recipe, you will see that the main difference is that we did not use the `beside` argument. By default, it is set to FALSE, which results in a stacked bar chart. We extended the top y axis limit from 100 up to 200.

There's more...

Another common use of stacked charts is to compare relative proportion of values across categories. Let's use the example dataset `citysalesperc.csv`, which contains the percentage values of sales data by city for each of the three products A, B, and C:

```
citysalesperc<-read.csv("citysalesperc.csv")

par(mar=c(5,4,4,8),xpd=T)

barplot(as.matrix(citysalesperc[,2:4]),
col=brewer.pal(5,"Set1"),border="white",
ylab="Sales Revenue (1,000's of USD)",
main="Percentage Sales Figures")

legend("right",legend=citysalesperc$City,bty="n",
inset=c(-0.3,0),fill=brewer.pal(5,"Set1"))
```

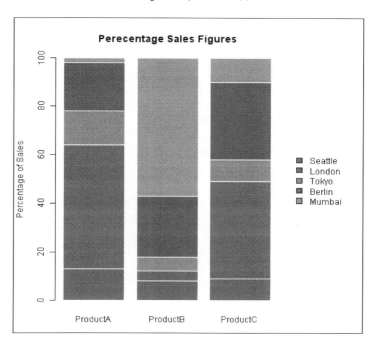

In the graph, the Y axis shows the percentage of sales of a product in a city. It is a good way to quickly visually compare the relative proportion of product sales in cities. The code we used for the main graph is the same as the previous example. One difference is that we drew the legend separately using the `legend()` command. Note that we drew the legend outside the plot region by setting the x part of inset to a negative value. We also had to create a larger margin to the right using the `mar` argument in the `par()` function and also setting `xpd` to `TRUE` to allow the legend to be drawn outside the plot region.

Adjusting the orientation of bars—horizontal and vertical

In this recipe, we will learn how to adjust the orientation of bars to horizontal or vertical.

Getting ready

We will use the same dataset we used in the last few recipes (`citysales.csv`) and the `RColorBrewer` color palette package.

How to do it...

Let's make a bar chart with horizontal bars:

```
barplot(as.matrix(citysales[,2:4]), beside=TRUE,horiz=TRUE,
legend.text=citysales$City, args.legend=list(bty="n"),
col=brewer.pal(5,"Set1"),border="white",
xlim=c(0,100), xlab="Sales Revenue (1,000's of USD)",
main="Sales Figures")
```

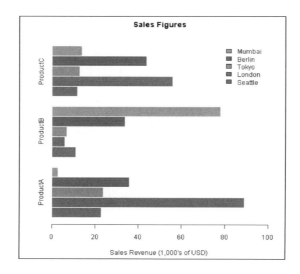

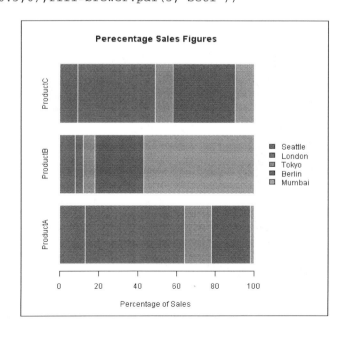

How it works...

In the example, we set the `horiz` argument to `TRUE`, which makes the bars horizontal. By default `horiz` is set to `FALSE`, making the bars vertical. While it's really easy to make the bars horizontal, we must remember that the axes are reversed when we do that. So, in the example, we had to set the limits for the X axis (`xlim` instead of `ylim`) and set `xlab` (instead of `ylab`) to `"Sales Revenue"`. We also removed the `horiz=TRUE` argument from the legend arguments list because that would have plotted some of the legend labels on top of the **ProductC** bars. Removing the `horiz` argument puts the legend back into its default top right position.

There's more...

Let's draw the stacked bar chart from the last recipe with horizontal bars:

```
par(mar=c(5,4,4,8),xpd=T)

barplot(as.matrix(citysalesperc[,2:4]), horiz=TRUE,
col=brewer.pal(5,"Set1"),border="white",
xlab="Percentage of Sales",
main="Perecentage Sales Figures")

legend("right",legend=citysalesperc$City,bty="n",
inset=c(-0.3,0),fill=brewer.pal(5,"Set1"))
```

Again, we had to simply set the `horiz` argument to `TRUE` and adjust the margins to accommodate the legend to the right outside the plot region.

Adjusting bar widths, spacing, colors, and borders

In this recipe, we will learn how to adjust the styling of bars by setting their width, the space between them, colors, and borders.

Getting ready

We will continue using the `citysales.csv` example dataset in this recipe. Make sure you have loaded it into R and type the recipe at the R prompt. You may also want to save the recipe as a script so that you can easily run it again later.

How to do it...

Let's adjust all the arguments at once to make the same graph as in the first recipe but with different visual settings:

```
barplot(as.matrix(citysales[,2:4]), beside=TRUE,
legend.text=citysales$City, args.legend=list(bty="n",horiz=T),
col=c("#E5562A","#491A5B","#8C6CA8","#BD1B8A","#7CB6E4"),
border=FALSE,space=c(0,5),
ylim=c(0,100),ylab="Sales Revenue (1,000's of USD)",
main="Sales Figures")
```

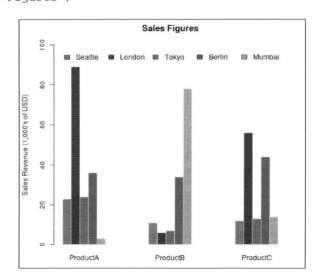

How it works...

Firstly, we changed the colors of the bars by setting the `col` argument to a vector of five colors we formed by hand, instead of using a `RColorBrewer` palette. If we do not set the `col` argument, R automatically uses shades from the grayscale.

Next, we set the `border` argument to `FALSE`. This tells R not to draw borders around each individual bar. By default black borders are drawn around bars, but they usually don't look very good. So, we set border to `"white"` in the earlier recipes of this chapter.

Finally, we set the `space` argument to `c(0,5)`, a vector of two numbers, to set the space between bars within each category and between the groups of bars representing each category respectively. We left no space between bars within a category and increased the space between categories.

Adjusting the space between bars automatically adjusts the width of the bars too. There is also a `width` argument, which we can use to set the width when plotting data for a single category, but the `width` argument is ignored when plotting for multiple categories. So, it's best to use `space` instead.

There's more...

The following is an example showing the previous graph with the default settings for color, spacing, and borders:

```
barplot(as.matrix(citysales[,2:4]), beside=T,
legend.text=citysales$City,args.legend=list(bty="n",horiz=T),
ylim=c(0,100),ylab="Sales Revenue (1,000's of USD)",
main="Sales Figures")
```

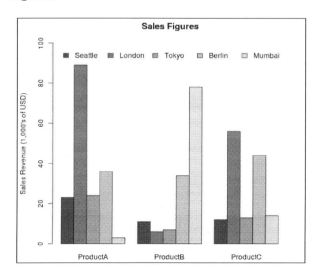

Displaying values on top of or next to the bars

Sometimes it is useful to have the exact values displayed on a bar chart to enable quick and accurate reading. There is no built-in function in R to do this. In this recipe, we will learn how to do this by writing some custom code.

Getting ready

Once again we will use the `citysales.csv` dataset and build upon the graph from the first recipe in this chapter.

How to do it...

Let's make the graph with vertical bars and display the sales values just on top of the bars:

```
x<-barplot(as.matrix(citysales[,2:4]), beside=TRUE,
legend.text=citysales$City, args.legend=list(bty="n",horiz=TRUE),
col=brewer.pal(5,"Set1"),border="white",
ylim=c(0,100),ylab="Sales Revenue (1,000's of USD)",
main="Sales Figures")

y<-as.matrix(citysales[,2:4])

text(x,y+2,labels=as.character(y))
```

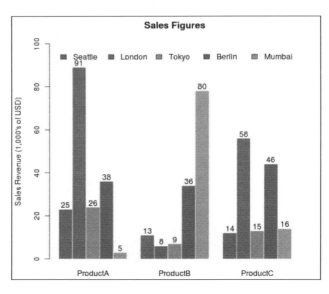

How it works...

In the example, we have used the `text()` function to label the bars with the corresponding values. To do so, we constructed two vectors `x` anc `y` with the X and Y co-ordinates of the labels. We first created the `barplot` and saved it as an R object called `x`. When the result of the `barplot()` function call is assigned to an object, a vector containing the X co-ordinates of the center of each of the bars is returned and saved in that object. You can verify this by typing `x` at the R prompt and hitting *Enter*.

For the `y` vector, we created a matrix of the sales value columns. Finally, we passed the `x` and `y` values to `text()` as co-ordinates and set the labels argument to `y` values transformed into characters using the `as.character()` function. Note that we added 2 to each `y` value so that the labels are placed slightly above the bar. We may have to add a different value depending on the scale of the graph.

There's more...

We can place the value labels next to the bars in a horizontal bar chart simply by swapping the `x` and `y` vectors in the `text()` function call:

```
y<-barplot(as.matrix(citysales[,2:4]), beside=TRUE,horiz=TRUE,
legend.text=citysales$City,args.legend=list(bty="n"),
col=brewer.pal(5,"Set1"),border="white",
xlim=c(0,100),xlab="Sales Revenue (1,000's of USD)",
main="Sales Figures")

x<-as.matrix(citysales[,2:4])

text(x+2,y,labels=as.character(x))
```

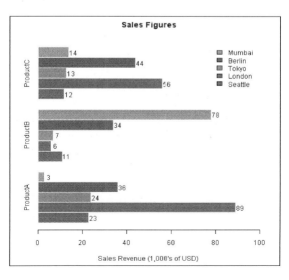

See also

In the next recipe, we will learn how to place text labels inside bars.

Placing labels inside bars

Sometimes we may wish to label bars by placing text inside the bars instead of using a legend. In this recipe, we will learn how to do that based on code similar to the previous recipe.

Getting ready

We will use the `cityrain.csv` example dataset. We don't need to load any additional packages for this recipe.

How to do it...

We will plot the rainfall in the month of January in four cities as a horizontal bar chart:

```
rain<-read.csv("cityrain.csv")

y<-barplot(as.matrix(rain[1,-1]),horiz=T,col="white",
yaxt="n",main=" Rainfall in January",xlab="Rainfall (mm)")

x<-0.5*rain[1,-1]
text(x,y,colnames(rain[-1]))
```

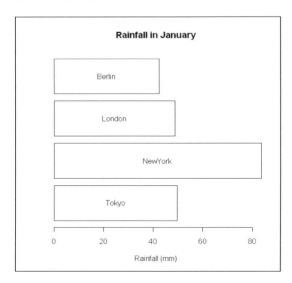

How it works...

The example is very similar to the one in the previous recipe. The only difference is that now we are plotting one set of bars, not groups of bars. Because we want to place the labels inside the bars, we turned off the Y axis labels by setting `yaxt="n"`. Otherwise, the city names would appear along the Y axis to the left of the bars. We retrieve the Y axis co-ordinates of the bars by setting `y` to the `barplot` function call. We created the vector `x` so as to place the labels in the middle of each of the bars by multiplying the rainfall values by `0.5`. Note that these X co-ordinates represent the center of each label, not its start. Finally, we pass the `x` and `y` co-ordinates and city names to `text()` to label the bars.

There's more...

As we have seen in the example and the previous recipe, once we retrieve the `x` or `y` co-ordinates of the center of bars, we can place labels in any position relative to those co-ordinates.

Creating bar charts with vertical error bars

Bar charts with error bars are commonly used in analysing and reporting results of scientific experiments. In this recipe, we will learn how to add error bars to a bar chart in a similar way to the recipe for scatter plots in *Chapter 3*.

Getting ready

We will continue using the `citysales.csv` example dataset in this recipe. Make sure you have loaded it into R and type the recipe at the R prompt. You may also want to save the recipe as a script so that you can easily run it again later.

How to do it...

One change we will make in this recipe is that we will use the transpose of the `citysales` dataset (turns rows into columns and columns into rows). So, first let's create the transpose as a new dataset:

```
sales<-t(as.matrix(citysales[,-1]))
colnames(sales)<-citysales[,1]
```

Now, let's make a bar plot with 5% error bars showing the sales of the three products across the five cities as categories:

```
x<-barplot(sales,beside=T,legend.text=rownames(sales),
args.legend=list(bty="n",horiz=T),
col=brewer.pal(3,"Set2"),border="white",ylim=c(0,100),
```

```
ylab="Sales Revenue (1,000's of USD)",
main="Sales Figures")

arrows(x0=x,y0=sales*0.95,
x1=x,y1=sales*1.05,
angle=90,
code=3,
length=0.04,
lwd=0.4)
```

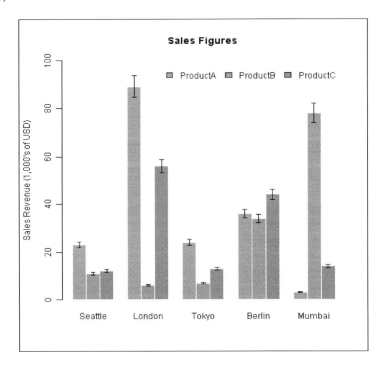

How it works...

We first created the bar chart with the transposed data, so that the sales data are represented as groups of three products for each of the cities. We saved the X co-ordinates of these bars as a vector x. Then we used the `arrows()` function, just like we used it in *Chapter 3* for making error bars on scatter plots. The first four arguments are the X and Y co-ordinate pairs of the start and end points of the error bars. The X co-ordinates x0 and x1 are both set equal to x and the Y co-ordinates are sales values 5% above and below the original values. The `angle` and `code` set the type of arrow and flatten the arrow head relative to the length of the arrow; `length` and `lwd` set the length and line width of the arrows.

There's more...

The code for drawing the error bars can be saved as a function and used with any `barplot`. This can be especially useful when comparing experimental values with control values, trying to look for a significant effect:

```
errorbars<-function(x,y,upper,lower=upper,length=0.04,lwd=0.4,...) {
arrows(x0=x,y0=y+upper,
x1=x,y1=y-lower,
angle=90,
code=3,
length=length,
lwd=lwd)
}
```

Now, error bars can be added to the previous graph' and delete 'can be drawn simply by calling:

```
errorbars(x,sales,0.05*sales)
```

In practice, scaled estimated standard deviation values or other formal estimates of error would be used for drawing error bars instead of a blanket percentage error as shown here.

Modifying dot charts by grouping variables

In this recipe, we will learn how to make dot charts with grouped variables. Dot charts are often preferred to bar charts because they are less cluttered and convey the same information more clearly with less ink.

Getting ready

We will continue using the `citysales.csv` example dataset in this recipe. Make sure you have loaded it into R and type the recipe at the R prompt. You may also want to save the recipe as a script so that you can easily run it again later. We will need the `reshape` package to change the structure of the dataset. So let's make sure we have it installed and loaded:

```
install.packages("reshape")
library(reshape)
```

How to do it...

We will first apply the `melt()` function to the `citysales` dataset to convert it to long form and then use the `dotchart()` function:

```
sales<-melt(citysales)

sales$color[sales[,2]=="ProductA"] <- "red"
sales$color[sales[,2]=="ProductB"] <- "blue"
sales$color[sales[,2]=="ProductC"] <- "violet"

dotchart(sales[,3],labels=sales$City,groups=sales[,2],
col=sales$color,pch=19,
main="Sales Figures",
xlab="Sales Revenue (1,000's of USD)")
```

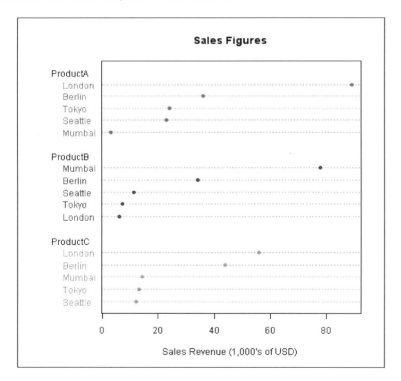

How it works...

We first converted the data into long form by applying the `melt()` function from the `reshape` library. The following is what the new dataset looks like:

City	Variable	Value
Mumbai	ProductA	3
London	ProductB	6
Tokyo	ProductB	7
Seattle	ProductB	11
Seattle	ProductC	12
Tokyo	ProductC	13
Mumbai	ProductC	14
Seattle	ProductA	23
Tokyo	ProductA	24
Berlin	ProductB	34
Berlin	ProductA	36
Berlin	ProductC	44
London	ProductC	56
Mumbai	ProductB	78
London	ProductA	89

Then we add a column called `color`, which holds a different value of color for each product (red, blue, and violet).

Finally we call the `dotchart()` function with the values column as the first argument. We set the `labels` argument to the city names and group the points by the second column (product). The color is set to the color column using the `col` argument. This results in a dot chart with the data points grouped and colored by products on the Y axis.

Making better readable pie charts with clockwise-ordered slices

Pie charts are very popular in business data reporting. However, they are not preferred by scientists and often criticized for being hard to read and obscuring data. In this recipe, we will learn how to make better pie charts by ordering the slices by size.

Getting ready

In this recipe, we will use the `browsers.txt` example dataset, which contains data about the usage percentage share of different internet browsers.

How to do it...

First we will load the `browsers.txt` dataset and then use the `pie()` function to draw a pie chart:

```
browsers<-read.table("browsers.txt",header=TRUE)
browsers<-browsers[order(browsers[,2]),]

pie(browsers[,2],
labels=browsers[,1],
clockwise=TRUE,
radius=1,
col=brewer.pal(7,"Set1"),
border="white",
main="Percentage Share of Internet Browser usage")
```

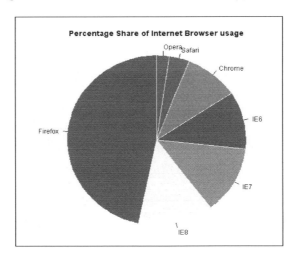

How it works...

The important thing about the graph is that the slices are ordered in ascending order of their sizes. We have done this because one of the main criticisms of pie charts is that when there are many slices and they are in a random order, it is not easy (often impossible) to tell whether one slice is bigger than another. By ordering the slices by size in a clockwise direction, we can directly compare the slices.

We ordered the dataset by using the `order()` function, which returns the index of its argument in ascending order. So if we just type `order(browsers[,2])` at the R prompt we get:

```
[1]  7 6 5 3 2 1 4
```

That's a vector of the index of the share values in ascending order in the original dataset. For example, Firefox which has the largest share is in the fourth row, so the last number in the vector is 4. We then use the index to reassign the `browser` dataset in the ascending order of share by using the square bracket notation.

Then we pass the share values in the second column as the first argument to the `pie()` function of the base R graphics library. We set labels to the first column, the names of browsers (note IE stands for Internet Explorer). We also set the `clockwise` argument to `TRUE`. By default slices are drawn counterclockwise.

See also

In the next two recipes, we will see how we can further enhance pie charts with percentage value labels.

Labelling a pie chart with percentage values for each slice

In this recipe, we will learn how to add the percentage values in addition to the names of slices, thus making them more readable.

Getting ready

Once again in this recipe, we will use the `browsers.txt` example dataset, which contains data about the usage percentage share of different internet browsers.

How to do it...

First we will load the `browsers.txt` dataset and then use the `pie()` function to draw a pie chart:

```
browsers<-read.table("browsers.txt",header=TRUE)
browsers<-browsers[order(browsers[,2]),]

pielabels <- sprintf("%s = %3.1f%s", browsers[,1],
100*browsers[,2]/sum(browsers[,2]), "%")

pie(browsers[,2],
labels=pielabels,
clockwise=TRUE,
radius=1,
```

```
col=brewer.pal(7,"Set1"),
border="white",
cex=0.8,
main="Percentage Share of Internet Browser usage")
```

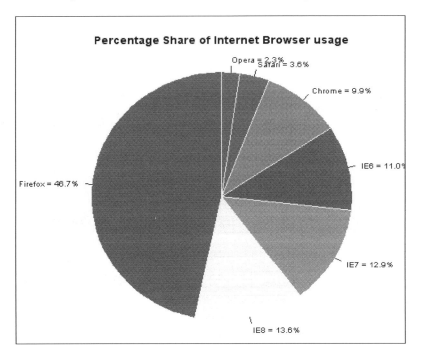

How it works...

In the example, instead of using just the browser names as labels, we first created a vector of labels which concatenated the browser names and percentage share values. We used the `sprintf()` function that returns a character vector containing a formatted combination of text and variable values. The first argument to `sprintf()` is the full character string in double quotes, where the `%` notation is used to fill in values dynamically and thus create a vector of strings for each slice. `%s` refers to a character string (`browsers[,1]` which is the second argument). `%3.1` refers to a three digit value with one significant decimal place (the percentage share value calculated as the third argument). The second `%s` refers to the character `"%"` itself, which is the last argument.

We make the pie chart using the same `pie()` function call as in the last recipe, except that we set `labels` to the newly constructed vector `pielabels`.

There's more...

We can adjust the size of the chart and the text labels by using the radius and cex arguments respectively.

See also

In the next recipe we will see how to add a legend to a pie chart.

Adding a legend to a pie chart

Sometimes we may wish to use a legend to annotate a pie chart instead of using labels. In this recipe we will learn how to do that using the legend() function.

Getting ready

Once again in this recipe, we will use the browsers.txt example dataset, which contains data about the usage percentage share of different internet browsers.

How to do it...

First we will load the browsers.txt dataset and then use the pie() function to draw a pie chart:

```
browsers<-read.table("browsers.txt",header=TRUE)
browsers<-browsers[order(browsers[,2]),]

pielabels <- sprintf("%s = %3.1f%s", browsers[,1],
100*browsers[,2]/sum(browsers[,2]), "%")

pie(browsers[,2],
labels=NA,
clockwise=TRUE,
col=brewer.pal(7,"Set1"),
border="white",
radius=0.7,
cex=0.8,
main="Percentage Share of Internet Browser usage")
```

```
legend("bottomright",legend=pielabels,bty="n",
fill=brewer.pal(7,"Set1"))
```

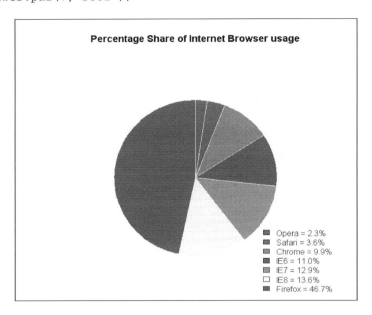

Percentage Share of Internet Browser usage

Opera = 2.3%
Safari = 3.6%
Chrome = 9.9%
IE6 = 11.0%
IE7 = 12.9%
IE8 = 13.6%
Firefox = 46.7%

How it works...

Once again we ordered the `browser` dataset, created a vector of labels and made the pie chart with the `pie()` function call, just like in the previous recipe. However, we set `labels` to `NA` this time as we want to create a legend instead of labeling the slices directly.

We added a legend to the bottom-right corner by calling the `legend()` function. We passed the `pielabels` vector as the `legend` argument and set the `fill` argument to the same `RColorBrewer` color palette we used for the pie slices.

There's more...

Depending on the number of slices and the desired size of the chart, we can experiment with placing the legend in different places. In this case, we have a lot of slice labels, otherwise we could place the legend in one single row on top of the chart by setting x to `"top"` and `horiz` to `TRUE`.

6
Creating Histograms

In this chapter, we will cover:

- ▶ Visualizing distributions as count frequencies or probability densities
- ▶ Setting bin size and number of breaks
- ▶ Adjusting histogram styles: bar colors, borders, and axes
- ▶ Overlaying density line over a histogram
- ▶ Multiple histograms along the diagonal of a pairs plot
- ▶ Histograms in the margins of line and scatter plots

Introduction

In this chapter, we will look in some detail at histograms, which are a very useful form of visualization to quickly see the distribution of values of a variable. They are usually one of the first graphs looked at to see whether a variable follows a normal distribution or has a skewed distribution.

We will see how we can enhance the basic histogram in R by adjusting some parameters in the base graphics library. We will learn how to change certain settings to control the format in which the histogram is plotted (frequency or probability of values) and also how the values are grouped into bins. We will also look at the usual parameters for changing the styling of histogram bars, such as color, width, and border. In addition, we will also look at some advanced recipes combining histograms with other types of graphs.

As with the previous chapters, it is best to try out each recipe first with the example shown here and then with your own datasets so that you can fully understand each line of code.

Visualizing distributions as count frequencies or probability densities

Histograms can represent the distribution of values either as frequency (the absolute number of times values fall within specific ranges) or as probability density (the proportion of the values that fall within specific ranges). In this recipe, we will learn how to choose one or the other.

Getting ready

We are only using base graphics functions for this recipe. So, just open up the R prompt and type the following code. We will use the `airpollution.csv` example dataset for this recipe. So let's first load it:

```
air<-read.csv("airpollution.csv")
```

How to do it...

We will use the base graphics function `hist()` to make our histogram, first showing frequency and then probability density of Nitrogen Oxide concentrations:

```
hist(air$Nitrogen.Oxides,
xlab="Nitrogen Oxide Concentrations",
main="Distribution of Nitrogen Oxide Concentrations")
```

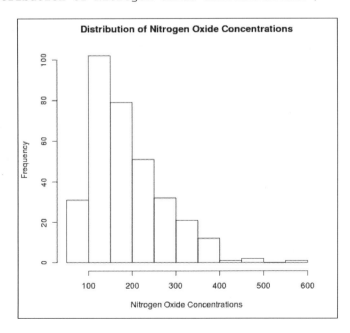

Now, let's make the same histogram but with probability instead of frequency:

```
hist(air$Nitrogen.Oxides, freq=FALSE,
xlab="Nitrogen Oxide Concentrations",
main="Distribution of Nitrogen Oxide Concentrations")
```

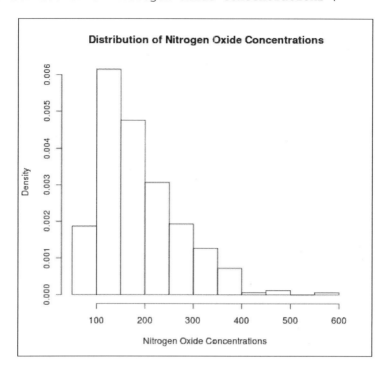

How it works...

The first example showing the frequency counts of different value ranges of Nitrogen Oxides simply uses a call to the hist() function in the base graphics library. The variable is passed as the first argument and by default the histogram plotted shows frequency. In the second example, we passed an extra argument freq and set it to FALSE, which results in a histogram showing probability densities. This suggests that by default freq is set to TRUE. The help section on hist() (?hist) states that freq defaults to TRUE if and only breaks are equidistant and probability is not specified.

There's more...

An alternative to using the freq argument is the prob argument, which as the name suggests takes the opposite value to freq. So, by default, it is set to FALSE and if we want to show probability densities then we need to set prob to TRUE.

Setting bin size and number of breaks

As we saw in the previous recipe, the `hist()` function automatically computes the number or breaks and size of bins in which to group the values of the variable. In this recipe, we will learn how we can control that and specify exactly how many bins we want or where to have breaks between bars.

Getting ready

Once again, we will use the `airpollution.csv` example dataset, so make sure you have loaded it:

```
air<-read.csv("airpollution.csv")
```

How to do it...

First, let's see how to specify the number of breaks. Let's make 20 breaks in the Nitrogen Oxides histogram instead of the default 11:

```
hist(air$Nitrogen.Oxides,
breaks=20,xlab="Nitrogen Oxide Concentrations",
main="Distribution of Nitrogen Oxide Concentrations")
```

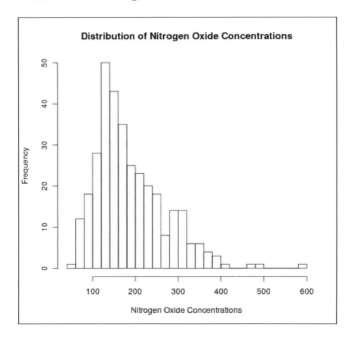

How it works...

We used the `breaks` argument to specify the number of bars for the histogram. We set `breaks` to `20`, however the graph shows more than 20 bars because R uses the value specified only as a suggestion and computes the best way to bin the data with breaks as close to the value specified as possible.

There's more...

We can also specify the exact values at which we want the breaks to occur. In this case, R does use the value we specify. Once again we use the `breaks` argument but this time we have to set it to a numerical vector containing the values at which we want the breaks. The `breaks` vector must cover the full range of values of the X variable.

Let's say we want breaks at every `100` units of concentration:

```
hist(air$Nitrogen.Oxides,
breaks=c(0,100,200,300,400,500,600),
xlab="Nitrogen Oxide Concentrations",
main="Distribution of Nitrogen Oxide Concentrations")
```

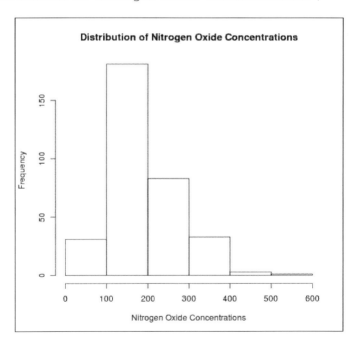

So, as you may have noticed, the `breaks` argument can take different types of values: a single value suggesting the number of breaks or a vector specifying exact bin breaks. In addition, `breaks` can also take a function which computes the number of bins.

Finally, `breaks` can also take a character string as value naming an algorithm to calculate the number of bins. By default, it is set to `"Sturges"`. Other names for which algorithms are supplied are `"Scott"` and `"FD"` or `"Freedman-Diaconis"`.

Adjusting histogram styles: bar colors, borders, and axes

The default styling of histograms does not look great and may not be suitable for publications. In this recipe, we will learn how to improve the look by setting bar colors, borders, and adjusting the axes.

Getting ready

Once again we will use the `airpollution.csv` example. So let's make sure it is loaded by running the following command at the R prompt:

```
air<-read.csv("airpollution.csv")
```

How to do it...

Let's visualize the probability distribution of Respirable Particle Concentrations with black bars and white borders:

```
hist(air$Respirable.Particles,
prob=TRUE,col="black",border="white",
xlab="Respirable Particle Concentrations",
main="Distribution of Respirable Particle Concentrations")
```

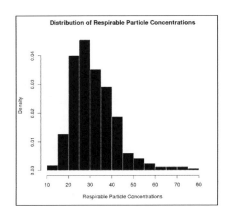

How it works...

By now you may have guessed how to do that yourself. We used the `col` and `border` arguments to set the bar and border colors to black and white respectively.

There's more...

You may have noticed that in all of the previous examples the X axis is detached from the base of the bars. This gives the graphs a bit of an unclean look. Also notice that the Y axis labels are rotated vertically, which makes them harder to read. Let's improve the graph by fixing these two visual settings:

```
par(yaxs="i",las=1)
hist(air$Respirable.Particles,
prob=TRUE,col="black",border="white",
xlab="Respirable Particle Concentrations",
main="Distribution of Respirable Particle Concentrations")
box(bty="l")
grid(nx=NA,ny=NULL,lty=1,lwd=1,col="gray")
```

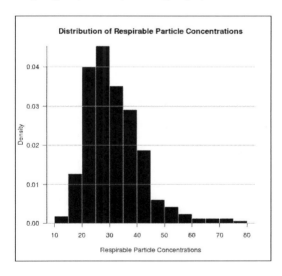

So we used a couple of extra function calls to change the look of the graph. First we called the `par()` function and set `yaxs` to `"i"` so that the Y axis joins the X axis instead of having a detached X axis. We also set `las` equal to `1` to make all the axis labels horizontal, thus making it easier to read the Y axis labels. Then we ran the `hist()` function call as before and called `box()` with type equal to `"l"` to make an L-shaped box running along the axes. Finally, we added horizontal grid lines using the `grid()` function.

Overlaying density line over a histogram

In this recipe we will learn how to superimpose a kernel density line on top of a histogram.

Getting ready

We will continue using the `airpollution.csv` example dataset. You can simply type the recipe code at the R prompt. If you wish to use the code later, you should save it as a script file. First, let's load the data file:

```
air<-read.csv("airpollution.csv")
```

How to do it...

Let's overlay a line showing the kernel density of Respirable Particle Concentrations on top of a probability distribution histogram:

```
par(yaxs="i",las=1)
hist(air$Respirable.Particles,
prob=TRUE,col="black",border="white",
xlab="Respirable Particle Concentrations",
main="Distribution of Respirable Particle Concentrations")
box(bty="l")

lines(density(air$Respirable.Particles,na.rm=T),col="red",lwd=4)
grid(nx=NA,ny=NULL,lty=1,lwd=1,col="gray")
```

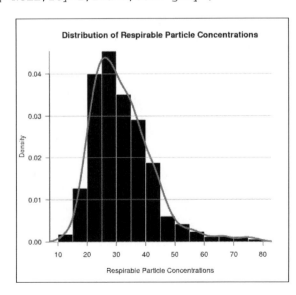

How it works...

The code for the histogram itself is exactly the same as in the previous recipe. After making the `hist()` function call, we used the `lines()` function to plot the density line on top. We passed the result of the `density()` function call to the `lines()` function. The default kernel used is gaussian, although other values can be specified. Please have a look at the help file for `density()` for more details (run `?density` at the R prompt).

To make the line prominent, we set its type to solid (`lty=1`), color to red (`col="red"`), and width to 4 (`lwd=4`).

Multiple histograms along the diagonal of a pairs plot

In this recipe, we will look at some slightly advanced code to embed histograms inside another kind of graph. We learnt how to make pairs plots (a matrix of scatter plots) in *Chapters 1* and *Chapter 3*. In those pairs plots, the diagonal cells running from the top-left to the bottom-right showed the names of the variables, while the other cells showed the relationship between any two pairs of variables. It would be useful if we could also see the probability distribution of each variable in the same plot. Here, we will learn how to do that by adding histograms inside the diagonal cells.

Getting ready

We will use the inbuilt iris flowers dataset of R. So we need not load any other datasets. We can simply type the given code at the R prompt.

How to do it...

So let's make an enhanced pairs plot showing the relationship between different measurements of the iris flower species and how each measurement's values are spread across the range:

```
panel.hist <- function(x, ...)
  {
    par(usr = c(par("usr")[1:2], 0, 1.5) )
    hist(x, prob=TRUE,add=TRUE,col="black",border="white")
  }
```

```
plot(iris[,1:4],
main="Relationships between characteristics of iris flowers",
pch=19,col="blue",cex=0.9,
diag.panel=panel.hist)
```

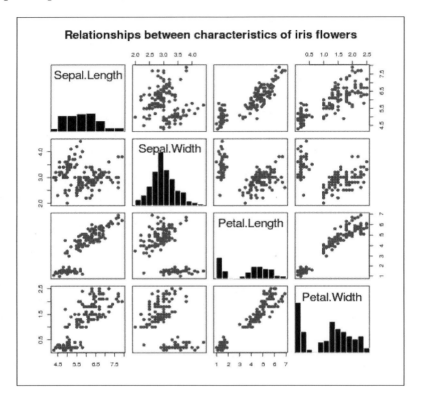

How it works...

We first defined the `panel.hist()` function which handles how the histograms are drawn. It is called by the `plot()` function later when the argument `diag.panel` is set to `panel.hist`.

The `panel.hist()` function only has two simple lines of code. First, we call the `par()` function to set the X and Y limits using the `usr` argument. To reiterate what we learnt in *Chapter 2*, the `usr` arguments takes values in the form of a vector `c(xmin,xmax,ymin,ymax)` giving the minimum and maximum values on the X and Y axes respectively. In the code, we keep the X axis limits the same as already set up by the `plot()` function call. We need to change the Y axis limits for each diagonal cell because they are set by `plot()` to be the same as the X axis limits. We need the Y axis limits in terms of the kernel density of each variable, so we set them to 0 and 1.5.

Then we make the `hist()` function call with the style arguments of our choice and one key argument `add` (set to `TRUE`), which makes sure the histograms are added to the existing pairs plot and not drawn as new plots. Any panel function should not start a new plot or it will terminate the pairs plot. So, we can't use the `hist()` function without setting `add` to `TRUE`.

Histograms in the margins of line and scatter plots

In this recipe, we will learn how to draw histograms in the top and right margins of a bivariate scatter plot.

Getting ready

We will use the `airpollution.csv` example dataset for this recipe. So, let's make sure it is loaded:

```
air<-read.csv("airpollution.csv")
```

How to do it...

Let's make a scatter plot showing the relationship between Concentrations of Respirable Particles and Nitrogen Oxides with histograms of both the variables in the margins:

```
#Set up the layout first
layout(matrix(c(2,0,1,3),2,2,byrow=TRUE), widths=c(3,1),
heights=c(1,3), TRUE)

#Make Scatterplot
par(mar=c(5.1,4.1,0.1,0))
plot(air$Respirable.Particles~air$Nitrogen.Oxides,
pch=19,col="black",
xlim=c(0,600),ylim=c(0,80),
xlab="Nitrogen Oxides Concentrations",
ylab="Respirable Particle Concentrations")

#Plot histogram of X variable in the top row
par(mar=c(0,4.1,3,0))
hist(air$Nitrogen.Oxides,
breaks=seq(0,600,100),ann=FALSE,axes=FALSE,
col="black",border="white")
```

```
#Plot histogram of Y variable to the right of the scatterplot
yhist <- hist(air$Respirable.Particles,
breaks=seq(0,80,10),plot=FALSE)

par(mar=c(5.1,0,0.1,1))
barplot(yhist$density,
horiz=TRUE,space=0,axes=FALSE,
col="black",border="white")
```

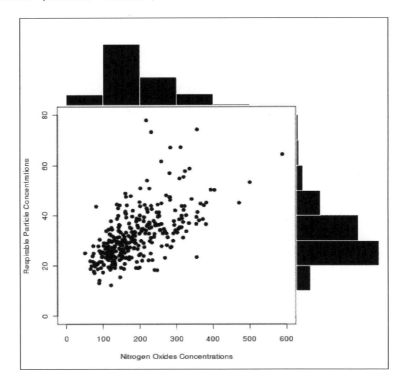

How it works...

The given example is a bit more complex than the recipes we have seen so far. However, if we look at each line of code one-by-one we can understand it quite easily.

First we used the `layout()` function to divide the graph into separate regions for the scatter plot and the two histograms. We could also use the `par()` function with the `mfrow` argument instead, but `layout()` gives us finer control over the height and width of each cell of the graph. When we use `par()` with `mfrow` or `mfcol` to create a matrix layout, all cells are automatically created of equal heights and widths.

The first argument to the `layout()` function is a matrix specifying the number of rows and columns the graphics device should be divided into and the location of each figure. Run just the matrix command from the code at the R prompt to see the resultant matrix:

```
matrix(c(2,0,1,3),2,2,byrow=TRUE)
     [,1] [,2]
[1,]   2    0
[2,]   1    3
```

The matrix values shown here mean that the first figure should be drawn in the second row and first column (scatter plot), the second figure in the first row and first column (histogram of X variable), and the third figure in the second row and second column (histogram of Y variable).

The other arguments to `layout()` are `widths` and `heights` which specify the widths and heights of the columns and rows respectively as a vector. The last argument is set to `TRUE` so that a unit column-width is the same physical measurement on the device as a unit row-height.

We have chosen this particular layout so that the scatter plot occupies most of the area of the graph and the histograms are plotted in a smaller area as they are only giving supplementary information.

Once the layout is created, we draw the plots one by one in the order that we set up the layout matrix. So, first we made the scatter plot giving specific X and Y axis limits, so that we can use the same limits to plot the histograms with the correct breaks.

Then we made the histogram of Nitrogen Oxides in the top margin just above the scatter plot. We first used the `par()` function with the `mar` argument to set the margins so as not to leave any margin at the bottom and matching the margins on the left and right to those of the scatter plot. We specified the `breaks` exactly as a vector of values between the X and Y limits of the scatter plot by using the `seq()` function. The axes and annotations are suppressed by setting the `axes` and `ann` arguments to `FALSE`, thus giving the histogram a clean minimal look.

Next, we added the rotated histogram of Respirable Particle Concentrations to the right of the scatter plot. We had to do this differently from the first histogram because the `hist()` function does not have an inbuilt way to draw the bars horizontally. As we have seen in earlier chapters, the `barplot()` function does have such a capability. So, we first created a histogram object but suppressed its plotting by setting the plot to `FALSE`. Then we passed the density values from that object to the `barplot()` function to plot them horizontally by setting the `horiz` argument to `TRUE`. Just like the X axis histogram, we set the breaks of the Y histogram equal to a sequence matching the Y limits of the scatter plot. Then we set the margins so that the bottom and top margins match those of the scatter plot and the left margin is zero. Then we called the `barplot()` function to draw the horizontal bars. Note that we set the `space` argument equal to zero, otherwise the bars are drawn with gaps between them by default.

7
Creating Box and Whisker Plots

In this chapter, we will cover:

- ▶ Creating box plots with narrow boxes for a small number of variables
- ▶ Grouping over a variable
- ▶ Varying box widths by number of observations
- ▶ Creating box plots with notches
- ▶ Including or excluding outliers
- ▶ Creating horizontal box plots
- ▶ Changing box styling
- ▶ Adjusting the extent of plot whiskers outside the box
- ▶ Showing the number of observations
- ▶ Splitting a variable at arbitrary values into subsets

Introduction

In this chapter, we will look in some depth at box and whisker plots, which are a great form of visualization to summarize large amounts of data by showing Tukey's five-number summary: minimum, lower-hinge, median, upper-hinge, and maximum. Box plots are a good way to spot outliers and compare the key statistics for different variables or groups.

We will learn various stylistic and structural variations on how to adjust box plots in R (using the basic `boxplot()` command). In addition to changing the look of our box plots, we will also learn how to add additional useful information to them. We will start by looking at some basic arguments to change individual aspects of a box plot and slowly move to more advanced recipes involving the use of multiple function calls and arguments to create more complex types of box plots.

As with the previous chapters, it is best to try out each recipe first with the example shown here and then with your own datasets so that you can fully understand each line of code.

Creating box plots with narrow boxes for a small number of variables

R automatically adjusts the widths of boxes in a box plot according to the number of variables. This works fine when we have a relatively large number of variables (more than four), but you may find that for a small number of variables the default boxes are too wide. In this recipe, we will learn how to make the boxes narrower.

Getting ready

We are only using the base graphics functions for this recipe. So, just open up the R prompt and type the following code. We will use the `airpollution.csv` example dataset for this recipe. So let's first load it:

```
air<-read.csv("airpollution.csv")
```

How to do it...

We want to make a box plot summarizing the two columns in our dataset: Respirable Particles and Nitrogen Oxides. If we simply use the `boxplot` command we get a box plot with very wide boxes:

```
boxplot(air,las=1)
```

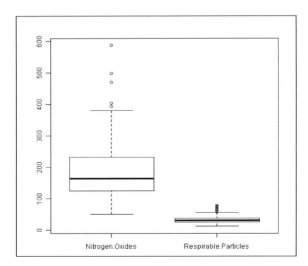

Let's improve the look of the graph by making the boxes narrower:

```
boxplot(air,boxwex=0.2,las=1)
```

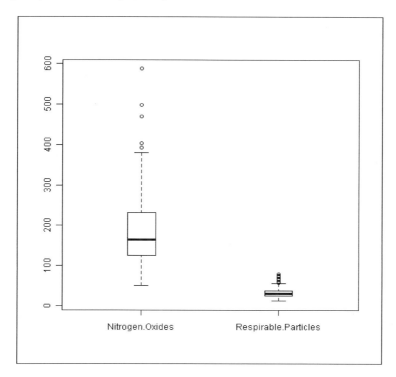

How it works...

So we changed the width of the boxes by passing the `boxwex` argument to the `boxplot()` command. We set `boxwex` to a value of `0.2`. The value depends on the number of variables we are plotting, but it should usually be less than `1`.

Note that we also passed the `las` argument with a value of `1` to make the Y axis labels horizontal. By default, they are parallel to the Y axis, thus making them difficult to read. Since we want this setting in all our graphs, we can set it globally by calling the `par()` function:

```
par(las=1)
```

 Note that we must not close the graphics device if we want to retain the setting. If we do close the device, we will need to set `las` to `1` again either using the `par()` function call or within each `boxplot()` function call. From now on, it is assumed that we will set `las` to `1` globally.

There's more...

Note that when we specify a width using `boxwex` the same value is applied to all the boxes in the plot. There is another argument, `width`, which can be used to set the relative widths of boxes. The `width` argument takes values in the form of a vector containing a value for each box. For example, if we wanted the box for Respirable Particles twice as wide as Nitrogen Oxides, we would run:

```
boxplot(air,width=c(1,2))
```

See also

Setting arbitrarily different widths for boxes using the `width` argument is not a good idea, unless the difference in widths conveys another important fact about the data. We will see one such example later in the chapter.

Grouping over a variable

In this recipe we will see how we can summarize data for a variable with respect to another variable in the dataset. We will learn to group over a variable such that a separate box plot is created for each group.

Getting ready

We are only using the base graphics functions for this recipe. So, just open up the R prompt and type the following code. We will use the `metals.csv` example dataset for this recipe. So let's first load it:

```
metals<-read.csv("metals.csv")
```

How to do it...

Let's make a box plot showing copper (Cu) concentrations grouped over measurement sites:

```
boxplot(Cu~Source,data=metals,
main="Summary of Copper (Cu) concentrations by Site")
```

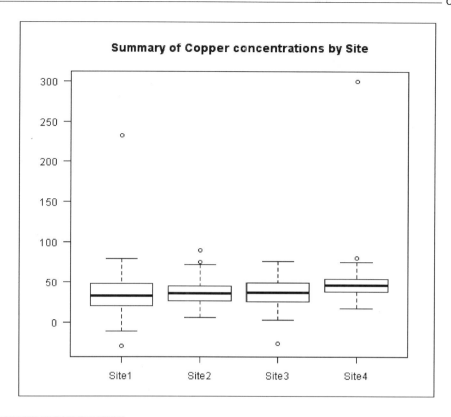

How it works...

The previous box plot works by using the formula notation `y~group`, where `y` is the variable whose values are depicted as separated box plots for each value of `group`.

There's more...

Grouping over a variable works well only when the group variable has a limited number of values, such as when it is a category (or factor in terms of an R data type) such as `Source` in this example. Grouping over another numerical variable with lots of unique values (say Manganese (Mn) concentrations) would result in a graph with too many box plots and not tell us much about the data.

We can also group over more than one category. If we wanted to group over the `Source` and another variable `Expt`, the experiment number, we could run:

```
boxplot(Cu~Source*Expt,data=metals,
main="Summary of Copper (Cu) concentrations by Site")
```

See also

We will use grouped box plots as examples in the next few recipes.

Varying box widths by number of observations

In this recipe, we will learn how to vary box widths in proportion to the number of observations for each variable.

Getting ready

Just like the previous recipe, we will continue to use the `metals.csv` example dataset for this recipe. So let's first load it:

```
metals<-read.csv("metals.csv")
```

How to do it...

Let's build a box plot with boxes of width proportional to the number of observations in the dataset:

```
boxplot(Cu ~ Source, data = metals,varwidth=TRUE,
main="Summary of Copper concentrations by Site")
```

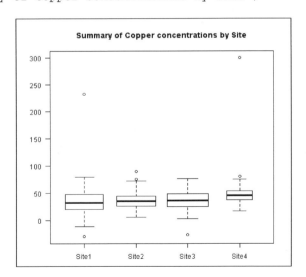

How it works...

In the example, we set the `varwidth` argument to `TRUE`, which makes the width of the boxes proportional to the square roots of the number of observations in the groups.

We can see that the box for **Site4** is the narrowest, since it has the least number of observations in the dataset. Differences in the other boxes' widths may not be so obvious, but this setting is useful when we are dealing with larger datasets. By default, `varwidth` is set to `FALSE`.

Creating box plots with notches

In this recipe, we will learn how to make box plots with notches, which are useful in comparing the medians of different groups.

Getting ready

We will continue to use the `metals.csv` example dataset for this recipe. So let's first load it:

```
metals<-read.csv("metals.csv")
```

How to do it...

We shall now see how to make a box plot with notches:

```
boxplot(Cu ~ Source, data = metals,
varwidth=TRUE,notch=TRUE,
main="Summary of Copper concentrations by Site")
```

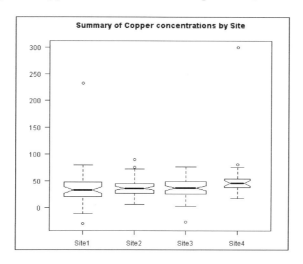

How it works...

In the example, we set the notch argument to TRUE to create notches on each side of the boxes. If the notches of two plots do not overlap, then the medians are significantly different at the 5% level, which suggests that the median concentrations at the four sites as shown are not statistically different from each other.

There's more...

We can set the notch.frac argument to a value between 0 and 1 to adjust the fraction of the box width that the notches should use. The default value is 0.5 and a value of 1 gives notches using the entire width of the box, effectively producing a box plot without notches.

Including or excluding outliers

In this recipe, we will learn how to remove outliers from a box plot. This is usually not a good idea because highlighting outliers is one of the benefits of using box plots. However, sometimes extreme outliers can distort the scale and obscure the other aspects of a box plot, so it is helpful to exclude them in those cases.

Getting ready

Let's continue using the metals.csv example dataset. So let's first make sure it's loaded:

```
metals<-read.csv("metals.csv")
```

How to do it...

Once again, we will use the base graphics boxplot() function with a specific argument to make our metal concentrations box plot without outliers:

```
boxplot(metals[,-1],outline=FALSE,
main="Summary of metal concentrations by Site \n
(without outliers)")
```

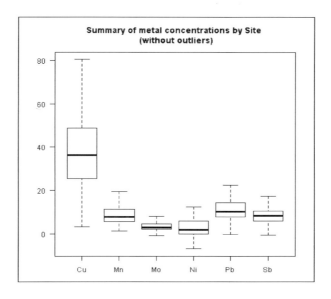

How it works...

We used the `outline` argument in the `boxplot()` function call to suppress the drawing of outliers. By default, `outline` is set to TRUE. To exclude outliers, we set it to FALSE.

See also

In the recipe *Adjusting the extent of plot whiskers outside the box*, later in the chapter, we will learn how to extend the whiskers of a box plot, which is another way of eliminating outliers by changing the definition of the cut-off value for an outlier.

Creating horizontal box plots

In this recipe, we will see how to make box plots with horizontal boxes instead of the default vertical ones.

Getting ready

We will continue using the base graphics library functions, so we need not load any additional package. We just need to run the recipe code at the R prompt. We can also save the code as a script to use it later. Here, we will use the `metals.csv` example dataset again:

```
metals<-read.csv("metals.csv")
```

How to do it...

Let's draw the metals concentration box plot with horizontal bars:

```
boxplot(metals[,-1],
horizontal=TRUE,las=1,
main="Summary of metal concentrations by Site")
```

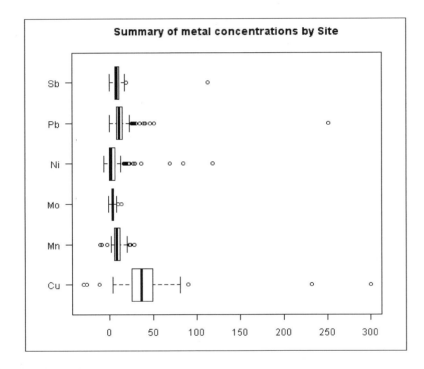

How it works...

We simply had to set the `horizontal` argument in the `boxplot()` command to `TRUE` to make the boxes horizontal. By default, it is set to `FALSE`.

 Note that unlike `barplots`, the argument name is `horizontal` and not just `horiz`.

Changing box styling

So far, we have used the default styling for our box plots. In this recipe, we will learn how to change the colors, widths, and styles of various elements of a box plot.

Getting ready

We will continue using the base graphics library functions, so we need not load any additional library or package. We just need to run the recipe code at the R prompt. We can also save the code as a script to use it later. Here, we will use the `metals.csv` example dataset again:

```
metals<-read.csv("metals.csv")
```

How to do it...

We can build a box plot with custom colors, widths, and styles in the following way:

```
boxplot(metals[,-1],
border = "white",col = "black",boxwex = 0.3,
medlwd=1, whiskcol="black",staplecol="black",
outcol="red",cex=0.3,outpch=19,
main="Summary of metal concentrations by Site")

grid(nx=NA,ny=NULL,col="gray",lty="dashed")
```

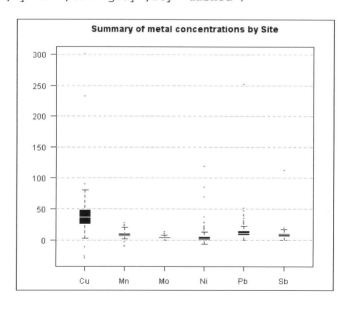

How it works...

We have used a few different arguments in the example to change the styling of the box plot. The first two are `col` and `border`, which set the box color and border color respectively. Note that the `border` argument also sets the color for the median line, unless it is specified using the `medcol` argument.

In the example, in addition to using `boxwex` for adjusting box widths, we used `medlwd` to set the width of the median line. We set the color of the whiskers and staple using `whiskcol` and `staplecol` respectively. The color and symbol type of the outlier points were set using `outcol` and `outpch` respectively. The size of the points was set using the `cex` argument.

There's more...

We can set the color, size, and styling for each of the components. If you type `?bxp` at the R prompt, you can see the help section for the `bxp()` function which is called by `boxplot()` to do the actual drawing. The following is a summary:

Argument to boxplot()	Corresponding setting
`boxlty, boxlwd, boxcol, boxfill`	Box outline type, width, color, and fill color
`medlty, medlwd, medpch, medcex, medcol, medbg`	Median line type, line width, point character, point size expansion, color, and background color
`whisklty, whisklwd, whiskcol`	Whisker line type, width, and color
`staplelty, staplelwd, staplewex, staplecol`	Staple line type, width, line width expansion, and color
`outlty, outlwd, outwex, outpch, outcex, outcol, outbg`	Outlier line type, line width, line width expansion, point character, point size expansion, color, and background color

Adjusting the extent of plot whiskers outside the box

Sometimes, we may wish to change the definition of outliers in our dataset by changing the extent of the whiskers. In this recipe, we will learn how to adjust the extent of whiskers in a box plot by passing a simple argument.

Getting ready

We will continue using the base graphics library functions, so we need not load any additional library or package. We just need to run the recipe code at the R prompt. We can also save the code as a script to use it later. Here, we will use the `metals.csv` example dataset again:

```
metals<-read.csv("metals.csv")
```

How to do it...

Let's draw the metal concentrations box plot with the whiskers closer to the box than the default one in the last recipe:

```
boxplot(metals[,-1],
range=1,border = "white",col = "black",
boxwex = 0.3,medlwd=1,whiskcol="black",
staplecol="black",outcol="red",cex=0.3,outpch=19,
main="Summary of metal concentrations by Site \n
(range=1) ")
```

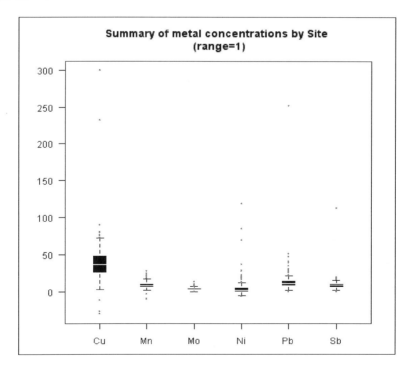

How it works...

We passed the `range` argument with a value of `1` to the `boxplot()` function in order to reduce the extent of the whiskers. The default value of `range` is `1.5`—it only takes positive values. The whiskers extend to the most extreme data point which is no more than range times the interquartile range from the box.

There's more...

If we want to extend the whiskers to the data extremes, we can either set `range` to a high enough value, such that range times the interquartile range from the box is more than the most extreme data point. Alternatively, we can simply set range to zero:

```
boxplot(metals[,-1],
range=0,border = "white",col = "black",
boxwex = 0.3,medlwd=1,whiskcol="black",
staplecol="black",outcol="red",cex=0.3,outpch=19,
main="Summary of metal concentrations by Site \n (range=0)")
```

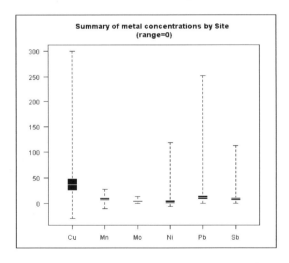

Showing the number of observations

It is often useful to know the number of observations for each variable or group when comparing them on a box plot. We did this earlier with the `varwidth` argument which makes the widths of boxes proportional to the square root of the number of observations. In this recipe, we will learn how to display the number of observations on a box plot.

Getting ready

We will continue using the base graphics library functions, so we need not load any additional library or package. We just need to run the recipe code at the R prompt. We can also save the code as a script to use it later. Here, we will use the `metals.csv` example dataset again:

```
metals<-read.csv("metals.csv")
```

How to do it...

Once again, let's use the metal concentrations box plot and display the number of observations for each metal below its label on the X axis:

```
b<-boxplot(metals[,-1],
xaxt="n",border = "white",col = "black",
boxwex = 0.3,medlwd=1,whiskcol="black",
staplecol="black",outcol="red",cex=0.3,outpch=19,
main="Summary of metal concentrations by Site")

axis(side=1,at=1:length(b$names),
labels=paste(b$names,"\n(n=",b$n,")",sep=""),
mgp=c(3,2,0))
```

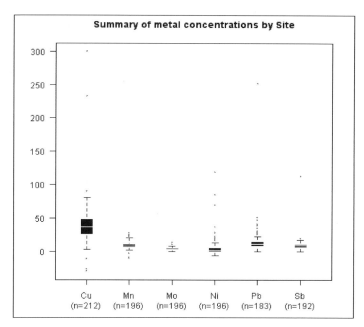

How it works...

In the example, we first made the same stylized box plot as we did two recipes ago, but we suppressed drawing the default X axis by setting xaxt to "n". We then used the axis() command to create our custom axis with the metal names and number of observations as labels.

We set side to 1 to denote the X axis. Note that we saved the object returned by the boxplot() function as b, which is a list containing useful information about the box plot. You can test this by typing b at the R prompt and hitting *Enter* (after you've run the boxplot command). We combined the names and n (number of observations) components of b using paste() to construct the labels argument. The at argument was set to integer values starting from 1 to the number of metals. Finally, we also used the mgp argument to set the margin line for the axis labels to 2, instead of the default 1, so that the extra line with number of observations doesn't make the labels overlap with the tick marks (you can see this if you omit mgp).

There's more...

Another way of displaying the number of observations on a box plot is to use the boxplot.n() function from the gplots package. First let's make sure the gplots package is installed and loaded:

```
install.packages("gplots")
library(gplots)

boxplot.n(metals[,-1],
border = "white",col = "black",boxwex = 0.3,
medlwd=1,whiskcol="black",staplecol="black",
outcol="red",cex=0.3,outpch=19,
main="Summary of metal concentrations by Site")
```

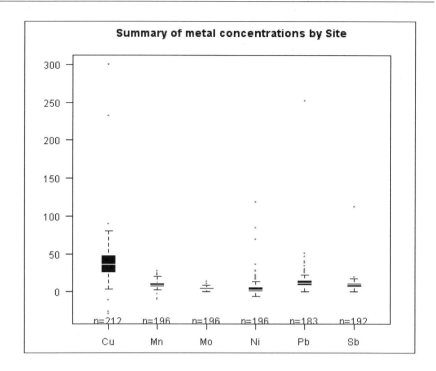

The problem with using this function is that the number labels are cut off by the axis. One way to get around this problem is to place the labels at the top of the plot region by setting the `top` argument to TRUE in the `boxplot.n()` function call.

Splitting a variable at arbitrary values into subsets

In this recipe, we will learn how to split a variable at arbitrary intervals of our choice to compare the box plots of values within each interval.

Getting ready

We will continue using the base graphics library functions, so we need not load any additional library or package. We just need to run the recipe code at the R prompt. We can also save the code as a script to use it later. Here, we will use the `metals.csv` example dataset again:

```
metals<-read.csv("metals.csv")
```

How to do it...

Let's make a box plot of copper (Cu) concentrations split at values 0, 40 and 80:

```
cuts<-c(0,40,80)
Y<-split(x=metals$Cu, f=findInterval(metals$Cu, cuts))

boxplot(Y,xaxt="n",
border = "white",col = "black",boxwex = 0.3,
medlwd=1,whiskcol="black",staplecol="black",
outcol="red",cex=0.3,outpch=19,
main="Summary of Copper concentrations",
xlab="Concentration ranges",las=1)

axis(1,at=1:length(clabels),
labels=c("Below 0","0 to 40","40 to 80","Above 80"),
lwd=0,lwd.ticks=1,col="gray")
```

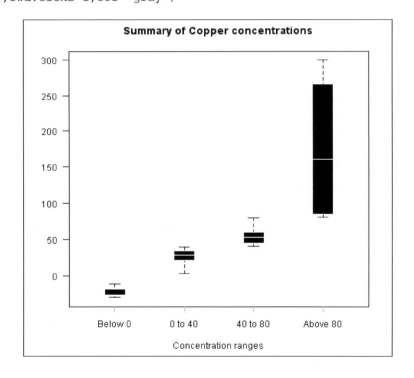

How it works...

We used a combination of a few different R functions to create the example graph shown. First, we defined a vector called `cuts` with values at which we wanted to cut our vector of concentrations. Then we used the `split()` function to split the copper concentrations vector into a list of concentration vectors at specified intervals (you can verify this by typing `Y` at the R prompt and hitting *Enter*). Note that we used the `findInterval()` function to create a vector of labels (factors) corresponding to the interval each value in `metals$Cu` lies in, and set the `f` argument of the `split()` function. Then we used the `boxplot()` function to create the basic box plot with the new `Y` vector and suppressed the default X axis. We then used the `axis()` function to draw the X axis with our custom labels.

There's more...

Let's turn the previous example into a function to which we can simply pass a variable and the intervals at which we wish to cut it, and it will draw the box plot accordingly:

```
boxplot.cuts<-function(y,cuts,...) {

    Y<-split(metals$Cu, f=findInterval(y, cuts))

    b<-boxplot(Y,xaxt="n",
    border = "white",col = "black",boxwex = 0.3,
    medlwd=1,whiskcol="black",staplecol="black",
    outcol="red",cex=0.3,outpch=19,
    main="Summary of Copper concentrations",
    xlab="Concentration ranges",las=1,...)


    clabels<-paste("Below",cuts[1])

    for(k in 1:(length(cuts)-1)) {
        clabels<-c(clabels, paste(as.character(cuts[k]),
        "to", as.character(cuts[k+1])))
    }

    clabels<-c(clabels,
    paste("Above",as.character(cuts[length(cuts)])))

    axis(1,at=1:length(clabels),
    labels=clabels,lwd=0,lwd.ticks=1,col="gray")

}
```

. . . is used to symbolize extra arguments to be added if required.

Now that we have defined the function, we can simply call it as follows:

```
boxplot.cuts(metals$Cu,c(0,30,60))
```

Another way to plot a subset of data in a box plot is by using the subset argument. For example, if we want to plot copper concentrations grouped by source above a certain threshold value (say 40), we can use:

```
boxplot(Cu~Source,data=metals,subset=Cu>40)
```

Note that we included an extra argument . . . to the definition of boxplot.cuts() in addition to y and cuts. This allows us to pass in any extra arguments which we don't explicitly use in the call to boxplot() inside the definition of our function. For example, if we can pass ylab as an argument to boxplot.cuts() even though it is not explicitly defined as an argument.

If you find this example too cumbersome (especially with the labels), following is an alternative definition of boxplot.cuts() which uses the cut() function and its automatic label creation:

```
boxplot.cuts<-function(y,cuts) {

    f=cut(y, c(min(y[!is.na(y)]),cuts,max(y[!is.na(y)])),
    ordered_results=TRUE);
    Y<-split(y, f=f)

    b<-boxplot(Y,xaxt="n",
    border = "white",col = "black",boxwex = 0.3,
    medlwd=1,whiskcol="black",staplecol="black",
    outcol="red",cex=0.3,outpch=19,
    main="Summary of Copper concentrations",
    xlab="Concentration ranges",las=1)


    clabels = as.character(levels(f))
    axis(1,at=1:length(clabels),
    labels=clabels,lwd=0,lwd.ticks=1,col="gray")

}
```

To create a box plot similar to the example shown earlier, we can run:

```
boxplot.cuts(metals$Cu,c(0,40,80))
```

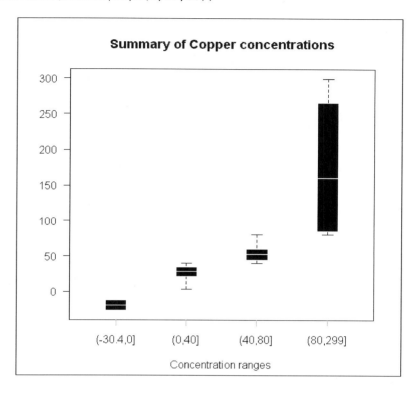

8

Creating Heat Maps and Contour Plots

In this chapter, we will cover:

- ▶ Creating heat maps of single Z variable with scale
- ▶ Creating correlation heat maps
- ▶ Summarizing multivariate data in a heat map
- ▶ Creating contour plots
- ▶ Creating filled contour plots
- ▶ Creating three-dimensional surface plots
- ▶ Visualizing time series as calendar heat maps

Introduction

In this chapter, we will learn how to make various types of heat maps and contour plots. By heat maps, we mean color coded grid images, useful for visualizing correlations, trends and multivariate data. We will see how contour plots can be used to show topographical information in various two-dimensional and three-dimensional ways.

The recipes in this chapter are a bit longer and more advanced than the ones in previous chapters. However, the code is clearly explained step by step, so that you can understand how it works.

As with the previous chapters, it is best to try out each recipe first with the example shown here and then with your own datasets so that you can fully understand each line of code.

Creating heat maps of single Z variable with scale

In this recipe we will learn how to make a heat map showing the variation in values of one variable (z) along the X and Y axes as a grid of colors, and display a scale alongside.

Getting ready

We are only using the base graphics functions for this recipe. So, just open up the R prompt and type the following code. We will use the `sales.csv` example dataset for this recipe. So let's first load it:

```
sales<-read.csv("sales.csv")
```

We will use the `RColorBrewer` package for some good color palettes. So let's make sure it's installed and loaded:

```
install.packages("RColorBrewer")
library(RColorBrewer)
```

How to do it...

The `sales` dataset has monthly sales data for four cities. Let's make a heat map with the months along the X axis and the cities on the Y axis:

```
rownames(sales)<-sales[,1]
sales<-sales[,-1]
data_matrix<-data.matrix(sales)

pal=brewer.pal(7,"YlOrRd")

breaks<-seq(3000,12000,1500)

#Create layout with 1 row and 2 columns (for the heatmap and scale);
the heatmap column is 8 times as wide as the scale column

layout(matrix(data=c(1,2), nrow=1, ncol=2), widths=c(8,1),
heights=c(1,1))

#Set margins for the heatmap
par(mar = c(5,10,4,2),oma=c(0.2,0.2,0.2,0.2),mex=0.5)


image(x=1:nrow(data_matrix),y=1:ncol(data_matrix),
```

```
z=data_matrix,axes=FALSE,xlab="Month",
ylab="",col=pal[1:(length(breaks)-1)],
breaks=breaks,main="Sales Heat Map")

axis(1,at=1:nrow(data_matrix),labels=rownames(data_matrix),
col="white",las=1)

axis(2,at=1:ncol(data_matrix),labels=colnames(data_matrix),
col="white",las=1)

abline(h=c(1:ncol(data_matrix))+0.5,
v=c(1:nrow(data_matrix))+0.5, col="white",lwd=2,xpd=FALSE)

breaks2<-breaks[-length(breaks)]

# Color Scale
par(mar = c(5,1,4,7))
# If you get a figure margins error while running the above code,
enlarge the plot device or adjust the margins so that the graph and
scale fit within the device.

image(x=1, y=0:length(breaks2),z=t(matrix(breaks2))*1.001,
col=pal[1:length(breaks)-1],axes=FALSE,breaks=breaks,
xlab="", ylab="",xaxt="n")

axis(4,at=0:(length(breaks2)-1), labels=breaks2, col="white",
las=1)

abline(h=c(1:length(breaks2)),col="white",lwd=2,xpd=F)
```

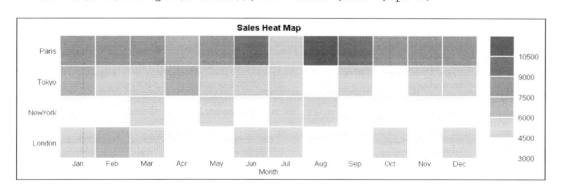

How it works...

We used a lot of steps and different function calls to create the heat map. Let's go through them one by one to understand how it all works.

Basically, we used the `image()` function in the base graphics library to create the heat map and its color scale. There is also a `heatmap()` function and a `heatmap.2()` function in the `gplots` package. However, we used `image()` because it is more flexible for our purpose.

First, we had to format the data in the correct format for `image()`, which requires that the z parameter be in the form of a matrix. The first column of the `sales` dataset contains the month names, which we assigned as the `rownames`. Then we removed the month column from the dataset and cast it as a matrix called `data_matrix`, containing only numerical values.

We defined `breaks` as a sequence of values from `3000` up to `12000` with steps of `1500`. These values are used to map the sales values to the color scale, where each color denotes values within a certain range. We used the `RColorBrewer` palette `YlOrRd` which contains seven warm colors.

We created a graph layout with one row and two columns using the `layout()` function. The left column for the heat map is eight times as wide as the right column for the color scale and their heights are equal.

We used the `image()` function to create the heat map. The main argument is z which we set to `data_matrix`. The x and y arguments take the index of the rows and columns of the matrix respectively. We set the `breaks` argument to the `breaks` vector we created earlier and set the `col` argument to our palette, but with the number of colors one less than the number of breaks. This is a requirement of the `image()` function.

Note that we suppressed the drawing of the default axes. We used the `axis()` command to draw the X and Y axes with row and column names respectively as the labels. The `abline()` function call is used to draw the white lines separating each block of color on the heat map (a bit like gridlines). These lines make the graph look nicer and a bit easier to read.

Finally, we drew the color scale by issuing another `image()` function call. We first created a subset of `breaks`, called `breaks2`, without the last element of `breaks`. We passed a transpose of a matrix of `breaks2` as the z argument to `image()`. Note that we also multiplied it by `1.001`, to create a set of values just above each break so that they are colored appropriately. We used the same `breaks` and `col` arguments as the heat map. We added a Y axis on side 4 to mark the break values and also used `abline()` to draw white horizontal lines to separate the breaks.

There's more...

The preceding code may seem a bit too complicated at first, but if you go through each statement and function call carefully, you will notice that it is just a big block of code with the same building blocks that we have used in earlier recipes. The best way to really understand the recipe and to modify it for your own needs is to change, add, or remove arguments from each function call and see the resulting effects.

See also

In the next few recipes, we will continue using the image() function to make some more types of heat maps.

Creating correlation heat maps

In this recipe, we will learn how to make a correlation heat map from a matrix of correlation coefficients.

Getting ready

We are only using the base graphics functions for this recipe. So, just open up the R prompt and type the following code. We will use the genes.csv example dataset for this recipe. So let's first load it:

```
genes<-read.csv("genes.csv")
```

How to do it...

Let's make a heat map showing the correlation between genes in a matrix:

```
rownames(genes)<-genes[,1]
data_matrix<-data.matrix(genes[,-1])

pal=heat.colors(5)

breaks<-seq(0,1,0.2)

layout(matrix(data=c(1,2), nrow=1, ncol=2), widths=c(8,1),
heights=c(1,1))

par(mar = c(3,7,12,2),oma=c(0.2,0.2,0.2,0.2),mex=0.5)

image(x=1:nrow(data_matrix),y=1:ncol(data_matrix),
z=data_matrix,xlab="",ylab="",breaks=breaks,
col=pal,axes=FALSE)
```

```
text(x=1:nrow(data_matrix)+0.75, y=par("usr")[4] + 1.25,
srt = 45, adj = 1, labels = rownames(data_matrix),
xpd = TRUE)

axis(2,at=1:ncol(data_matrix),labels=colnames(data_matrix),
col="white",las=1)

abline(h=c(1:ncol(data_matrix))+0.5,v=c(1:nrow(data_matrix))+0.5,
col="white",lwd=2,xpd=F)

title("Correlation between genes",line=8,adj=0)

breaks2<-breaks[-length(breaks)]

# Color Scale
par(mar = c(25,1,25,7))
image(x=1, y=0:length(breaks2),z=t(matrix(breaks2))*1.001,
col=pal[1:length(breaks)-1],axes=FALSE,
breaks=breaks,xlab="",ylab="",
xaxt="n")

axis(4,at=0:(length(breaks2)),labels=breaks,col="white",las=1)
abline(h=c(1:length(breaks2)),col="white",lwd=2,xpd=F)
```

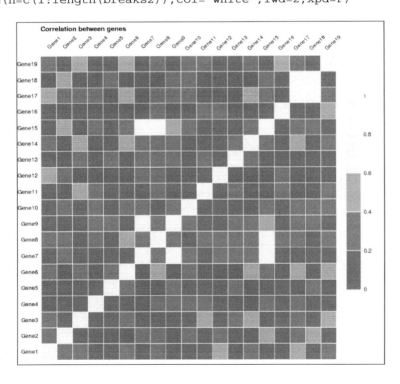

How it works...

Just like in the previous recipe, first we format the data using the first column values as row names and cast the dataframe as a matrix. We created a palette of five colors using the `heat.colors()` function and defined a sequence of breaks 0, 0.2, 0.4,...1.0.

Then we created a layout with one row and two columns (one for the heat map and the other for the color scale). We created the heat map using the `image()` command in a similar way to the previous recipe passing the data matrix as the value of the `z` argument.

We added custom X axis labels using the `text()` function, instead of the `axis()` function to rotate the axis labels. We also placed the labels in the top margin instead of the bottom margin as usual to improve the readability of the graph. This way it resembles a gene correlation matrix of numbers more closely, where the names of the genes are shown on the top and left. To create the rotated labels, we set the `srt` argument to `45`, thus setting the angle of rotation to 45 degrees.

Finally, we added a color scale to the right of the heat map.

There's more...

We can use a more contrasting color scale to differentiate between the correlation values. For example, to highlight the diagonal values of 1 more clearly, we can substitute the last color in our palette with white.

 If you get a figure margins error while running the code, enlarge the plot device or adjust the margins so that the graph and scale fit within the device.

Summarizing multivariate data in a heat map

In the preceding couple of recipes, we have looked at representing a matrix of data along two axes on a heat map. In this recipe, we will learn how to summarize multivariate data using a heat map.

Getting ready

We are only using the base graphics functions for this recipe. So, just open up the R prompt and type the following code. We will use the `nba.csv` example dataset for this recipe. So let's first load it:

```
nba <- read.csv("nba.csv")
```

This example dataset showing some statistics on the top scorers in NBA basketball games has been taken from a blog post on **FlowingData** (see `http://flowingdata.com/ 2010/01/21/how-to-make-a-heatmap-a-quick-and-easy-solution/` for details). The original data is from the **databaseBasketball.com** website (`http:// databasebasketball.com/`). We will use our own code to create a similar heat map showing player statistics.

We will use the `RColorBrewer` library for a nice color palette, so let's load it:

```
library(RColorBrewer)
```

How to do it...

We are going to summarize a number of NBA player statistics in the same heat map using the `image()` function:

```
rownames(nba)<-nba[,1]

data_matrix<-t(scale(data.matrix(nba[,-1])))

pal=brewer.pal(6,"Blues")

statnames<-c("Games Played", "Minutes Played", "Total Points",
"Field Goals Made", "Field Goals Attempted",
"Field Goal Percentage", "Free Throws Made",
"Free Throws Attempted", "Free Throw Percentage",
"Three Pointers Made", "Three Pointers Attempted",
"Three Point Percentage", "Offensive Rebounds",
"Defensive Rebounds", "Total Rebounds", "Assists", "Steals",
"Blocks", "Turnovers", "Fouls")

par(mar = c(3,14,19,2),oma=c(0.2,0.2,0.2,0.2),mex=0.5)

#Heat map
image(x=1:nrow(data_matrix),y=1:ncol(data_matrix),
z=data_matrix,xlab="",ylab="",col=pal,axes=FALSE)

#X axis labels
text(1:nrow(data_matrix), par("usr")[4] + 1,
srt = 45, adj = 0,labels = statnames,
xpd = TRUE, cex=0.85)

#Y axis labels
axis(side=2,at=1:ncol(data_matrix),
labels=colnames(data_matrix),
col="white",las=1, cex.axis=0.85)

#White separating lines
abline(h=c(1:ncol(data_matrix))+0.5,
```

```
v=c(1:nrow(data_matrix))+0.5,
col="white",lwd=1,xpd=F)

#Graph Title
text(par("usr")[1]+5, par("usr")[4] + 12,
"NBA per game performance of top 50corers",
xpd=TRUE,font=2,cex=1.5)
```

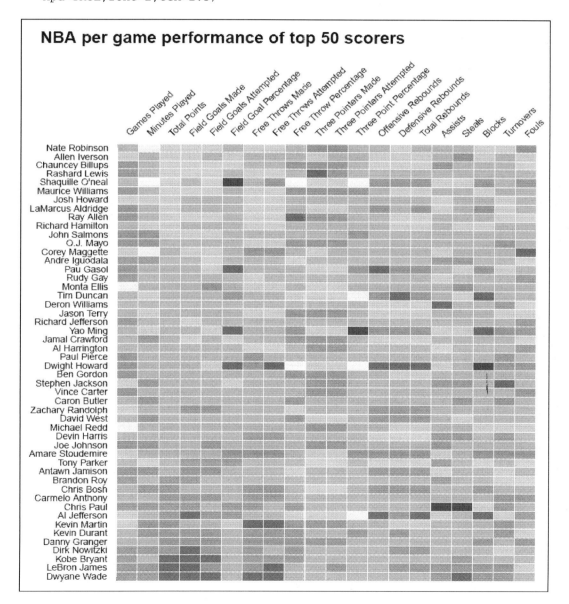

How it works...

Once again, in a way similar to the preceding couple of recipes, we first formatted the dataset with the appropriate row names (in this case names of players) and cast it as a matrix. We did one additional thing—we scaled the values in the matrix using the `scale()` function, which centers and scales each column so that we can denote the relative values of each column on the same color scale.

We chose a blue color palette from the `RColorBrewer` library. We also created a vector with the descriptive names of the player statistics to use as labels for the X axis.

The code for the heat map itself and the axis labels is very similar to the previous recipe. We used the `image()` function with `data_matrix` as z and suppressed the default axes. Then we used `text()` and `axis()` for adding the X and Y axis labels. We also used the `text()` function to add the graph title (instead of the `title()` function) in order to left-align it with the Y axis labels instead of the heat map.

There's more...

As shown in the **FlowingData** blog post, we can order the data in the matrix as per the values in any one column. By default, the data is in ascending order of total points scored by each player (as can be seen from the light to dark blue progression in the **Total Points** column). To order the players based on their scores from highest to lowest, we need to run the following code after reading the CSV file:

```
nba <- nba[order(nba$PTS),]
```

 See the help on the `order()` function by running `?order` or `help(order)` at the R prompt.

Then we can run the rest of the code to make the following graph:

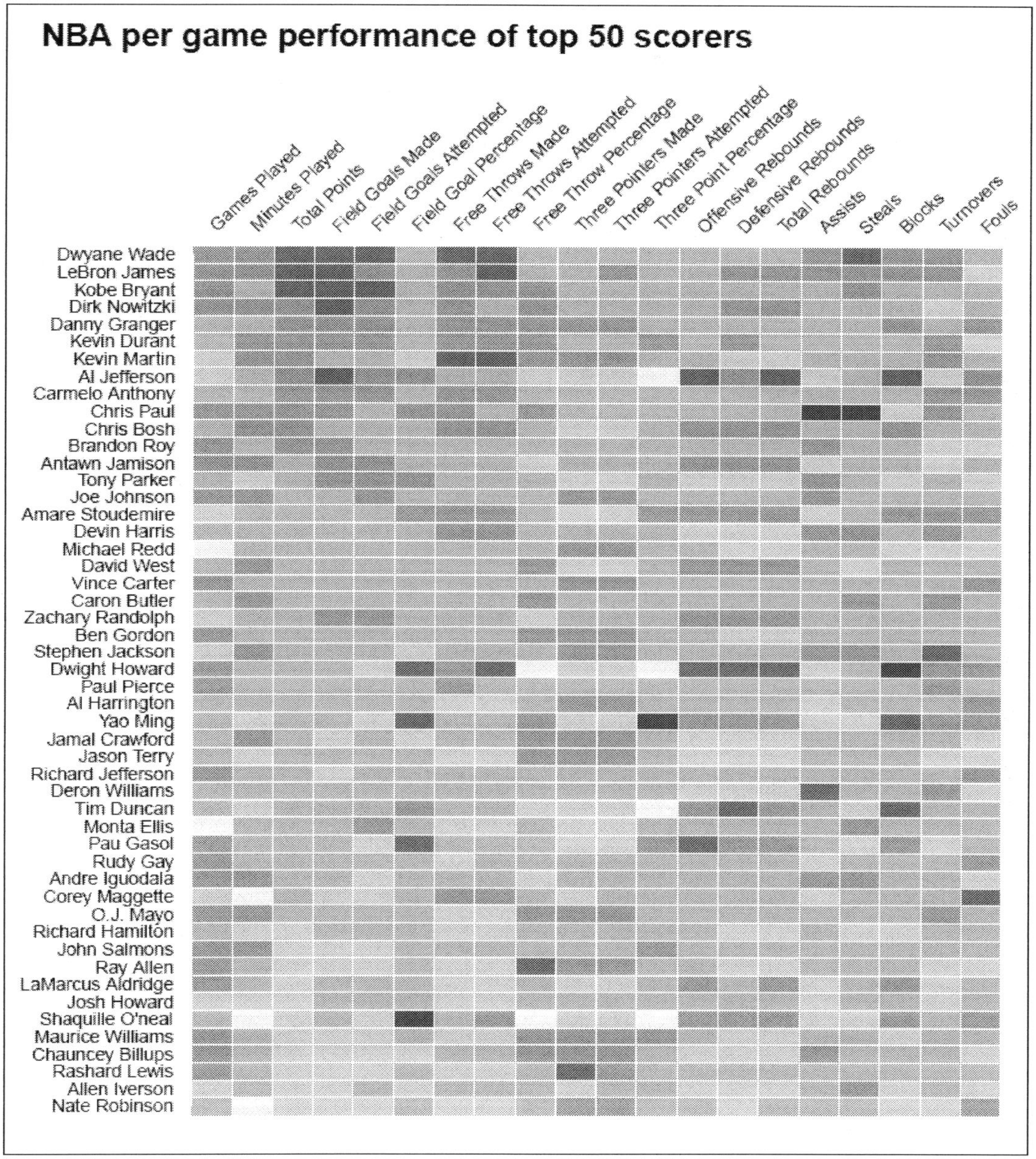
NBA per game performance of top 50 scorers
Games Played
Minutes Played
Total Points
Field Goals Made
Field Goals Attempted
Field Goal Percentage
Free Throws Made
Free Throws Attempted
Free Throw Percentage
Three Pointers Made
Three Pointers Attempted
Three Point Percentage
Offensive Rebounds
Defensive Rebounds
Total Rebounds
Assists
Steals
Blocks
Turnovers
Fouls
Dwyane Wade
LeBron James
Kobe Bryant
Dirk Nowitzki
Danny Granger
Kevin Durant
Kevin Martin
Al Jefferson
Carmelo Anthony
Chris Paul
Chris Bosh
Brandon Roy
Antawn Jamison
Tony Parker
Joe Johnson
Amare Stoudemire
Devin Harris
Michael Redd
David West
Vince Carter
Caron Butler
Zachary Randolph
Ben Gordon
Stephen Jackson
Dwight Howard
Paul Pierce
Al Harrington
Yao Ming
Jamal Crawford
Jason Terry
Richard Jefferson
Deron Williams
Tim Duncan
Monta Ellis
Pau Gasol
Rudy Gay
Andre Iguodala
Corey Maggette
O.J. Mayo
Richard Hamilton
John Salmons
Ray Allen
LaMarcus Aldridge
Josh Howard
Shaquille O'neal
Maurice Williams
Chauncey Billups
Rashard Lewis
Allen Iverson
Nate Robinson

Creating contour plots

In this recipe we will learn how to make contour plots to visualize topographical data, such as the terrain near a mountain or a volcano.

Getting ready

We are only using the base graphics functions for this recipe. So, just open up the R prompt and type the code we are about to see. We will use the inbuilt `volcano` dataset, so we need not load anything.

How to do it...

Let's first make a default contour plot using the `volcano` dataset:

```
contour(x=10*1:nrow(volcano), y=10*1:ncol(volcano), z=volcano,
xlab="Metres West",ylab="Metres North",
main="Topography of Maunga Whau Volcano")
```

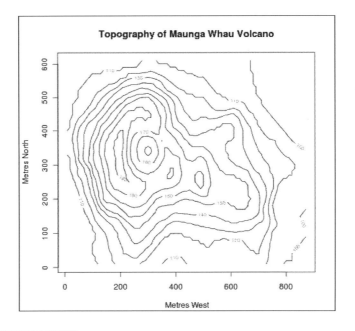

How it works...

We used the base graphics library function `contour()` to make the graph.

The arguments x and y specify the locations of the grid at which the height values (z) are specified. The `volcano` dataset contains topographic information on a 10X10 m grid, so we set the x and y grid arguments to 10 times the index numbers of rows and columns respectively.

The contour data z is provided by the `volcano` dataset in a matrix form.

The graph shows the height of the region in the form of contour lines, which outline all areas with the same height. The height for each contour line is shown in gray.

There's more...

Now let's improve the graph by making the Y axis labels horizontal and adding some colors to the plot area and contour lines:

```
par(las=1)

plot(0,0,xlim=c(0,10*nrow(volcano)),ylim=c(0,10*ncol(volcano)),
type="n",xlab="Metres West",
ylab="Metres North",main="Topography of Maunga Whau Volcano")

u<-par("usr")

rect(u[1],u[3],u[2],u[4],col="lightgreen")

contour(x=10*1:nrow(volcano),y=10*1:ncol(volcano),
volcano,col="red",add=TRUE)
```

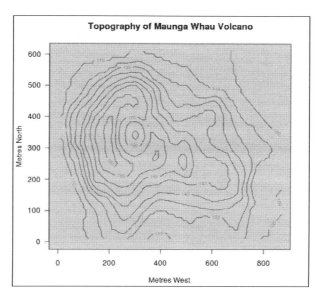

See also

In the next recipe, we will learn how to make filled contour plots, which use solid color to make the graph even easier to read.

Creating filled contour plots

In this recipe, we will learn how to make a contour plot with the areas between the contours filled in solid color.

Getting ready

We are only using the base graphics functions for this recipe. So, just open up the R prompt and type the code we are about to see. We will use the inbuilt `volcano` dataset, so we need not load anything.

How to do it...

Let's make a filled contour plot showing the terrain data of the Maunga Whau volcano in R's inbuilt `volcano` dataset:

```
filled.contour(x = 10*1:nrow(volcano),y = 10*1:ncol(volcano),
z = volcano, color.palette = terrain.colors,
plot.title = title(main = "The Topography of Maunga Whau",
xlab = "Meters North",ylab = "Meters West"),
plot.axes = {axis(1, seq(100, 800, by = 100))
             axis(2, seq(100, 600, by = 100))},
key.title = title(main="Height\n(meters)"),
key.axes = axis(4, seq(90, 190, by = 10)))
```

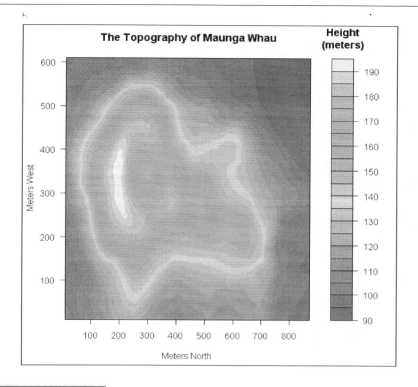

How it works...

If you type ?filled.contour you will see that the preceding example is taken from that help file (see the second example at the end of the help file). The filled.contour() function creates a contour plot with the areas between the contour lines filled with solid colors. In this case, we chose the terrain.colors() function to use a color palette suitable for showing geographical elevations. We set the color.palette argument to terrain.colors and the filled.contour() function automatically calculates the number of color levels.

The basic arguments are the same as those for contour(), namely, x and y that specify the locations of the grid at which the height values (z) are specified. The contour data z is provided by the volcano dataset in a matrix form.

The filled.contour() function is slightly different from other basic graph functions because it automatically creates a layout with the contour plot and key. We can't suppress or customize the styling of the key to a great extent. Also, some of the standard graph parameters have to be passed to other functions. For example, the axis labels xlab and ylab have to be passed as arguments to the title() function which is passed as the value for the plot.title argument. We cannot directly pass xlab and ylab to filled.contour().

We also have to add our custom axes by setting the `plot.axes` argument to a list of function calls to the `axis()` function. Unlike other functions, we cannot simply set `axes` to `FALSE` and call `axis()` after drawing the graph because of the internal use of `layout()` in `filled.contour()`. If we add axes after calling `filled.contour()`, the X axis will extend beyond the contour plot up to the key.

Finally, we set the title and tick labels of the key using the `key.title` and `key.axes` arguments respectively. Once again, we had to set these arguments to function calls to `title()` and `axis()` respectively instead of directly specifying the values.

There's more...

We can adjust the level of detail and smoothness between the contours by increasing their number using the `nlevels` argument:

```
filled.contour(x = 10*1:nrow(volcano),
y = 10*1:ncol(volcano), z = volcano,
color.palette = terrain.colors,
plot.title = title(main = "The Topography of Maunga Whau",
xlab = "Meters North",ylab = "Meters West"),nlevels=100,
plot.axes = {axis(1, seq(100, 800, by = 100))
             axis(2, seq(100, 600, by = 100))},
key.title = title(main="Height\n(meters)"),
key.axes = axis(4, seq(90, 190, by = 10)))
```

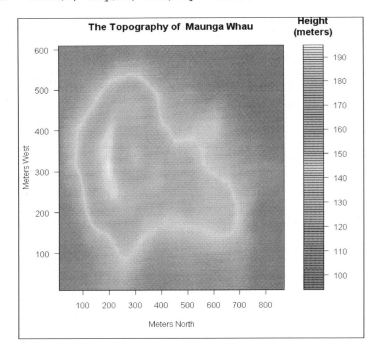

Note that there are a lot more contours now and the plot looks a lot smoother. The default value of `nlevels` is `20`, so we increased it by 5 times. The key doesn't look very nice because of too many black lines between each tick mark; however, as pointed out earlier, we cannot control that without changing the definition of the `filled.contour()` function itself.

See also

In the next recipe, we will learn how to make a three-dimensional version of a filled contour plot.

Creating three-dimensional surface plots

In this recipe, we will use a special library to make a three-dimensional (3D) surface plot for the `volcano` dataset. The resulting plot will also be interactive so that we can rotate the visualization using a mouse to look at it from different angles.

Getting ready

For this recipe, we will use the `rgl` package, so we must first install and load it:

```
install.packages("rgl")
library(rgl)
```

We will only use the inbuilt `volcano` dataset, so we need not load any other dataset.

How to do it...

Let's make a simple three-dimensional surface plot showing the terrain of the Maunga Whau volcano:

```
z <- 2 * volcano
x <- 10 * (1:nrow(z))
y <- 10 * (1:ncol(z))

zlim <- range(z)
zlen <- zlim[2] - zlim[1] + 1

colorlut <- terrain.colors(zlen)
col <- colorlut[ z-zlim[1]+1 ]

rgl.open()
rgl.surface(x, y, z, color=col, back="lines")
```

The 3D surface will look like following:

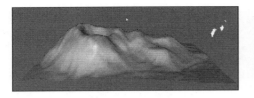
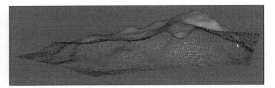

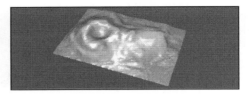

How it works...

RGL is a 3D real-time rendering device driver system for R. We used the `rgl.surface()` function to create the preceding visualization. Please see the help section (by running `?rgl.surface` at the R prompt) to see the original example at the bottom of the help file, on which the example is based.

We basically used the `volcano` dataset that we used in the previous couple of recipes and created a three-dimensional representation of the volcano's topography instead of the two-dimensional contour representation.

We set up the `x`, `y`, and `z` arguments in a similar way to the contour examples, except that we multiplied the volcano height data in `z` by 2 to exaggerate the terrain which helped us appreciate the library's 3D capabilities better.

Then we defined a matrix of colors for each point in `z` such that each height value has a unique color from the `terrain.colors()` function. We saved the mapped color data in `col` (if you type `col` at the R prompt and hit *Return* (or *Enter*), you will see that it contains 5,307 colors).

Then we opened a new RGL device with the `rgl.open()` command. This brings up a blank window with a gray background. Finally, we called the `rgl.surface()` function with the `x`, `y`, `z`, and `color` arguments. We also set the `back` argument to `"lines"`, which resulted in a wire-framed polygon underneath the visualization.

Once `rgl.surface()` is run, we can rotate the visualization using our mouse in any direction. This lets us look at the volcano from any angle. If we look underneath, we can also see the wire-frame. The images show snapshots of the volcano from four different angles.

There's more...

The example is a very basic demonstration of the `rgl` package's functionality.

There are a number of other functions and settings we can use to create a lot more complex visualizations customized to our needs. For example, the `back` argument can be set to other values to create a filled, point, or hidden polygon. We can also set the transparency (or opacity) of the visualization using the `alpha` argument. Arguments controlling the appearance of the visualization are sent to the `rgl.material()` function which sets the material properties.

Please read the related help sections (`?rgl`, `?rgl.surface`, `?rgl.material`) to get a more in-depth understanding of this library.

Visualizing time series as calendar heat maps

In this recipe, we will learn how to make intuitive heat maps in a calendar format to summarize time series data.

Getting ready

In this recipe, we will use a custom function called `calendarHeat()` written by Paul Bleicher (released as open source under the GPL license). So let's first load the source code of the function (available from the downloads area of the book's website):

```
source("calendarHeat.R")
```

We are going to use the `google.csv` example dataset, which contains stock price data for Google (ticker GOOG). Let's load it:

```
stock.data <- read.csv("google.csv")
```

`calendarHeat()` also make use of the `chron` library, which has to be installed and loaded using the following:

```
install.packages("chron")
library("chron")
```

How to do it...

Let's visualize the adjusted closing price of the Google stock in a calendar heat map:

```
calendarHeat(dates=stock.data$Date,
values=stock.data$Adj.Close,
varname="Google Adjusted Close")
```

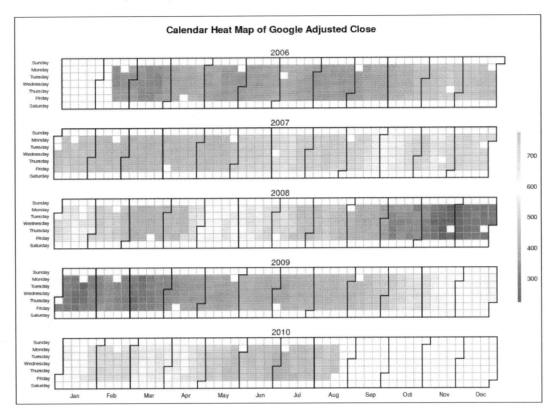

How it works...

We used the `calendarHeat()` function, which uses the `grid`, `lattice`, and `chron` libraries, to make the heat map. The main arguments are `dates` and `values`, which we set to the `Date` and `Adj.Close` columns of our dataset respectively. We also used the `varname` argument to set the title of the heat map.

There are several other arguments which can be passed to `calendarHeat()`. For example, we can specify the format our input dates are in using the `date.form` argument. The default format is YYYY-MM-DD, which matches our original dataset. However, if the dates were in another format, say MM-DD-YY, we could set `date.form` to `"%m-%d-%y"`.

The number of colors in the color scale are controlled by the `ncolors` argument, which has a default value of `99`. The color scheme is specified by the `color` argument, which takes some predefined palette names as values. The default is `r2g` (red to green), and other options are `r2b` (red to blue) and `w2b` (white to blue). We can add more options simply by adding a definition for a new color palette as a vector of colors.

There's more...

Another useful package which provides a calendar heat map functionality is the `openair` package, which has been primarily created for air pollution data analysis. Let's make a pollution heat map using this package.

First, we need to install and load it:

```
install.packages("openair")
library(openair)
```

To make our first air pollution calendar heat map, we can simply run:

```
calendarPlot(mydata)
```

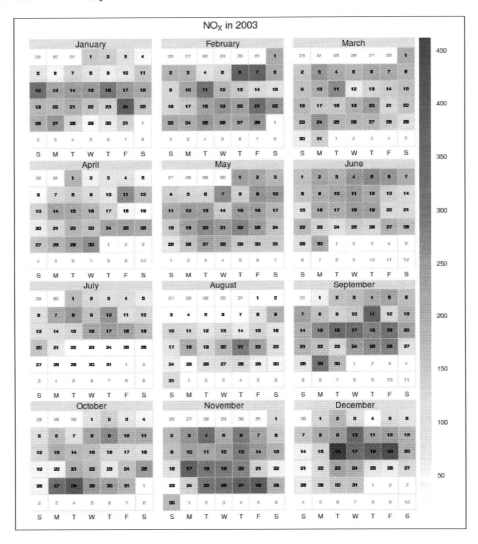

The graph shows some Nitrogen Oxides (NOx) concentration data from London in 2003 in the form of a heat map overlaid on a regular calendar.

We only had to pass one argument `mydata` to the `calendar.plot()` function, which uses the package's default `mydata` dataset. Run `head(mydata)` at the R prompt to see what the data looks like and all the columns in the dataset. The first column contains GMT date and time values in a long format (YYYY-MM-DD HH:MM:SS). If we want to use the `calendar.plot()`

function, as it is for visualizing other types of temporal data, we can do so as long as the date column is in the same format and we specify the variable to be plotted using the pollutant argument. The default value of pollutant is "nox", which is the name of the column that contains the NOx values.

Let's say, we want to plot daily sales data instead. Let's use the rnorm() function to create some fake data and add it as a column to the mydata dataset:

```
mydata$sales<-rnorm(length(mydata$nox),mean=1000,sd=1500)
```

The code added a sales column to mydata, with random values following a normal distribution with a mean of 1000 and standard deviation of 1500. Now, let's use calendar.plot() to make a heat map for this sales data.

```
calendarPlot(mydata,pollutant="sales",main="Daily Sales in 2003")
```

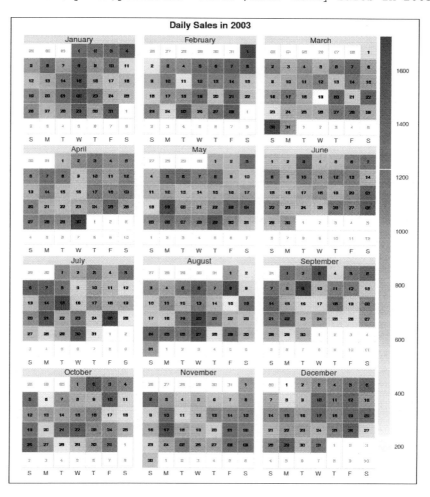

In the example, we set the `pollutant` argument to the newly created `sales` column (note that we have to pass it as a string in quotes). We also set the plot title using the `main` argument. The `calendar.plot()` function uses the `lattice` library to generate the heat maps. Please see the help file (`?calendar.plot`) to see other arguments you can use.

9
Creating Maps

In this chapter, we will cover:

- ▸ Plotting global data by countries on a world map
- ▸ Creating graphs with regional maps
- ▸ Plotting data on Google maps
- ▸ Creating and reading KML data
- ▸ Working with ESRI shapefiles

Introduction

In this chapter, we will take a more in-depth look at visualizing data on geographical maps, building on top of our brief introduction in *Chapter 1*.

Overlaying datasets from different parts of the world on maps is a very good way of summarizing data in its correct geographical context. A lot of data is being made freely available. For example, the World Bank and World Health Organization (WHO) publish lots of socio-economic and health-related data, which can be plotted on maps. Google Maps provides a good API, which can be directly connected to from R as we will see in this chapter.

We will also learn how to work with **Geographical Information Systems** (**GIS**) data formats in R.

As with the previous chapters, it is best to try out each recipe first with the example shown here and then with your own datasets so that you can fully understand each line of code.

Plotting global data by countries on a world map

In this recipe we will learn how to plot country-wise data on a world map.

Getting ready

We will use a few different additional packages for this recipe. We need the `maps` package for the actual drawing of the maps, the `WDI` package to get world bank data by countries, and the `RColorBrewer` package for color schemes. So let's make sure these packages are installed and loaded:

```
install.packages("maps")
library(maps)
install.packages("WDI")
library(WDI)
install.packages("RColorBrewer")
library(RColorBrewer)
```

How to do it...

There are a lot of different data we can pull in using the world bank API provided by the `WDI` package. In this example, let's plot some CO2 emissions data:

```
colors = brewer.pal(7,"PuRd")
wgdp<-WDIsearch("gdp")
w<-WDI(country="all", indicator=wgdp[4,1], start=2005, end=2005)

w[63,1] <- "USA"

x<-map(plot=FALSE)

x$measure<-array(NA,dim=length(x$names))

for(i in 1:length(w$country)) {
    for(j in 1:length(x$names)) {
        if(grepl(w$country[i],x$names[j],ignore.case=T))
            x$measure[j]<-w[i,3]
    }
}
```

```
sd <- data.frame(col=colors,
values <- seq(min(x$measure[!is.na(x$measure)]),
max(x$measure[!is.na(x$measure)]) *1.0001,
length.out=7))

sc<-array("#FFFFFF",dim=length(x$names))

for (i in 1:length(x$measure))
    if(!is.na(x$measure[i]))
        sc[i]=as.character(sd$col[findInterval(x$measure[i],
        sd$values)])

#2-column layout with color scale to the right of the map
layout(matrix(data=c(2,1), nrow=1, ncol=2), widths=c(8,1),
heights=c(8,1))

# Color Scale first
breaks<-sd$values

par(mar = c(20,1,20,7),oma=c(0.2,0.2,0.2,0.2),mex=0.5)

image(x=1, y=0:length(breaks),z=t(matrix(breaks))*1.001,
col=colors[1:length(breaks)-1],axes=FALSE
breaks=breaks,xlab="",ylab="",xaxt="n")

axis(side=4,at=0:(length(breaks)-1),
labels=round(breaks),col="white",las=1)

abline(h=c(1:length(breaks)),col="white",lwd=2,xpd=F)

#Map
map(col=sc,fill=TRUE,lty="blank")
# If you get a figure margins error while running the above code,
enlarge the plot device or adjust the margins so that the graph and
scale fit within the device.


map(add=TRUE,col="gray",fill=FALSE)
title("CO2 emissions (kg per 2000 US$ of GDP)")
```

The map plot of CO2 emissions looks like the following:

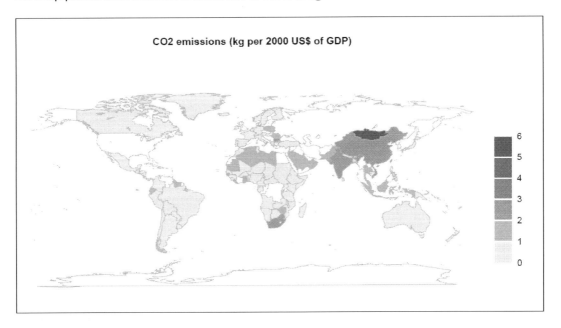

How it works...

We used the maps package in combination with world bank data from the WDI package above to plot CO2 emissions data per 2.000 US$ of GDP for various countries across the world.

First we chose an RColorBrewer color scheme and saved it as a vector called colors. We then pulled a list of GDP-related variables using the WDIsearch() function. If you type wgdp at the R prompt and hit *Enter*, you will see a list of codes and descriptions of each of these variables. For the previous example, we chose the fourth variable (wgdp[4,1]), which gives CO2 emissions (kg per 2.000 US$ of GDP), and passed it to the WDI() function to get data for all countries for the year 2005 by setting the country argument to "all" and start and end to 2005.

Next, we created a map object x simply by calling the map() function and setting plot to FALSE, so that the map is not drawn yet. We did this so that we can map the data we pulled from WDI to the country polygons contained in the map object.

First we added a new array called measure to x, with NA as default values and length matching the number of country names in x. If you type x$names at the R prompt and hit *Enter*, you will see the whole list of country names. Similarly, w$country contains the names of the countries for which the WDI package has data. Note that the map object has a lot more names because it contains regional information at a finer detail than just countries. So, we must first match the names of countries in the two datasets.

For the example, we use a simple search function `grepl()`, which looks for the WDI country names in the map object x and assigns the corresponding CO2 emissions values from w to x$measure. This is a very approximate solution and misses on countries where the names in the two datasets are not the same. For example, the United States is named USA in the WDI dataset. To match all the countries exactly, we need to manually check the important ones we are interested in. In the example, the United States was corrected manually.

Next we created a data frame called sd to define a color scheme with intervals based on a sequence from the minimum to the maximum values in x$measure. We use sd to assign a color for each of the values in x$measure by creating a vector called sc. First we create sc with default values of white, so that any missing values are depicted without any color. Then we used the `findInterval()` function to assign a color to each value of x$measure.

Finally, we have all the ingredients for making the map. We first used the `layout()` function to create a 1X2 layout just like we did for heat maps in the previous chapter.

We need to plot the color scale first here because if we plot the map first, the scale cannot be plotted on the same layout and results in a new plot with just the scale. We reversed this plotting order by setting the data argument in `layout()` to c(2,1) instead of c(1,2).

The color scale is drawn in exactly the same way as in the previous chapter for heat maps, using the `image()` function. To draw the map itself, we used the `map()` function. We set the col argument to the vector sc which contains colors corresponding to each polygon on the map. We set fill to TRUE and lty to "blank", so that we get the polygons filled with the specified colors and no blank borders around them. Instead, we add gray borders by calling the `map()` function with add set to TRUE, col set to gray and fill set to FALSE. Finally, we added a plot title using the `title()` function.

There's more...

The example shows just one variable for one year visualized on a map. The world bank package gives 73 different metrics related to GDP alone (as can be seen in the wgdp variable). See the help section for the WDI package for more details about other data available (?WDI and ?WDIsearch). If you have any other data by country from another source, you can use that with the `map()` function in the example as long as the country names can be matched to the names of regions in the map object.

See also

In the next recipe, we will learn how to plot regional data on individual country maps instead of on a world map.

Creating graphs with regional maps

In this recipe we will learn how to plot data on regional maps within individual countries rather than the whole world map. We will look at examples based on the United States and European countries.

Getting ready

Just like the previous recipe, we will make use of the `maps` package for drawing the map and the `RColorBrewer` package for choosing color schemes. So, let's make sure they are loaded:

```
library(maps)
library(RColorBrewer)
```

We will use the inbuilt `USArrests` example dataset, which contains crime statistics, in arrests per 100,000 residents for assault, murder, and rape in each of the 50 US states in 1973.

How to do it...

Let's plot the arrests rate for murders in US states in 1973. The default graphics device size may not be big enough for the map, so if you get an error about figure margins, please enlarge the graphics device:

```
x<-map("state",plot=FALSE)

for(i in 1:length(rownames(USArrests))) {
    for(j in 1:length(x$names)) {
        if(grepl(rownames(USArrests)[i],x$names[j],ignore.case=T))
            x$measure[j]<-as.double(USArrests$Murder[i])
    }
}

colors <- brewer.pal(7,"Reds")

sd <- data.frame(col=colors,
values=seq(min(x$measure[!is.na(x$measure)]),
max(x$measure[!is.na(x$measure)])*1.0001,
length.out=7))

breaks<-sd$values

matchcol<-function(y) {
    as.character(sd$col[findInterval(y,sd$values)])
```

```
}

layout(matrix(data=c(2,1), nrow=1, ncol=2),
widths=c(8,1), heights=c(8,1))

# Color Scale first
par(mar = c(20,1,20,7),oma=c(0.2,0.2,0.2,0.2),mex=0.5)
image(x=1, y=0:length(breaks),z=t(matrix(breaks))*1.001,
col=colors[1:length(breaks)-1],axes=FALSE,breaks=breaks,
xlab="", ylab="", xaxt="n")
axis(4,at=0:(length(breaks)-1),
labels=round(breaks),col="white",las=1)
abline(h=c(1:length(breaks)),col="white",lwd=2,xpd=F)

#Map
map("state", boundary = FALSE,col=matchcol(x$measure),
fill=TRUE,lty="blank")

map("state", col="white",add = TRUE)

title("Murder Rates by US State in 1973 \n
(arrests per 100,000 residents)", line=2)
```

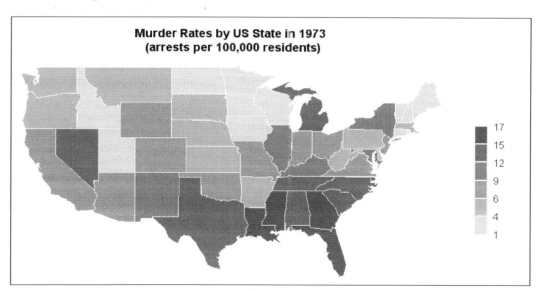

How it works...

The example is similar to the previous recipe in its overall structure, but it differs mainly in the fact that we plotted data for one country's states. We used the `USArrests` dataset, which is inbuilt in R and contains various crime figures by state for the United States.

Just like the previous recipe we first mapped the values of the chosen statistic (murder rates in this case) to the corresponding region names (in this case states) in the `map` object created using the `map()` function. We chose a red color scheme from `RColorBrewer`.

Instead of creating a vector of colors for each of the values plotted, we defined a function `matchcol()` which takes a value as an argument and uses the `findInterval()` function to return a color value from the data frame `sd` which contains the breaks and corresponding colors from the chosen palette.

We then created a two column layout and drew the color scale first in the right column. Then we plotted the map with `fill` set to `TRUE` and `col` set to a function call to `matchcol()` with `x$measure` as the argument. We set the boundary to `FALSE`, to draw white boundaries instead of the default black ones. We did so by calling `map()` again with `col` set to `white` and `add` set to `TRUE`. Finally, we used the `title()` function to add a map title.

There's more...

Mapping data by states is just one of the options in the `maps` package for the United States. We can also map data by counties and regions defined as groups of specific states. For example, we can draw a county map of New York with:

```
map("county", "new york")
```

Or we can draw a map with three states with:

```
map("state", region = c("california", "oregon", "nevada"))
```

Now let's look at another example, this time from a European country:

```
map('italy', fill = TRUE, col = brewer.pal(7,"Set1"))
```

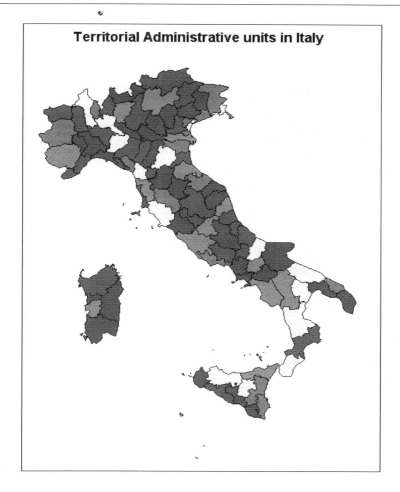

Territorial Administrative units in Italy

The preceding example uses the inbuilt dataset for Italy in the `maps` package. We used the colors just to differentiate the various territorial units from each other; the colors do not represent any numerical quantity. The `maps` package does not have geographical data for other countries. But there is one good source for world-wide geographical data: the GADM database of Global Administrative Areas. One can freely download data for countries across the world in R's native RData format for non-commercial use from the website `http://gadm.org`.

The GADM data can be used in combination with the `sp` package to plot regional data on maps. Let's look at an example of rainfall in France. First let's make sure the `sp` package is installed and loaded:

```
install.packages("sp")
library(sp)
```

Now let's create some pseudo rainfall data for the French administrative regions and plot it on a map of France:

```
load(url("http://gadm.org/data/rda/FRA_adm1.RData"))

gadm$rainfall<-rnorm(length(gadm$NAME_1),mean=50,sd=15)

spplot(gadm,"rainfall",
col.regions = rev(terrain.colors(gadm$rainfall)),
main="Rainfall (simulated) in French administrative regions")
```

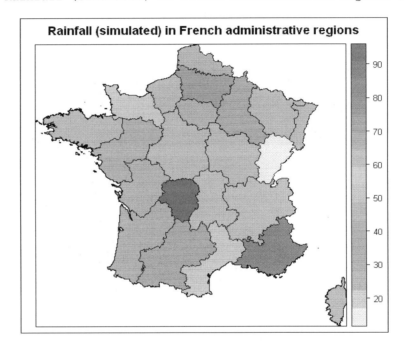

First we loaded the geographical boundary data for France by calling the `load()` function with a `url` of the location of the dataset on the GADM website. In this case, the dataset loaded was `FRA_adm1.RData`. This function call stores the data in an object called `gadm` (you can verify this by typing `gadm` at the R prompt and hitting *Enter*). Next, we appended a vector of pseudo rainfall data to `gadm` by calling the `rnorm()` function.

Finally, we used the `spplot()` function from the `sp` package to plot the data. The first argument to `spplot()` is the object `gadm` itself and the second argument is the name of the variable we wish to plot on the map. We set the fill color of the regions using `col.region`; this is slightly different from the `map()` function because the `sp` package is based on the `lattice` library. We used a color scheme based on the `terrain.colors()` function, but reversed it with `rev()` so that low to high rainfall is represented by gray through brown to green.

Plotting data on Google maps

In this recipe, we will learn how to plot data on top of Google map images using a special package that connects to Google's Static Maps API.

Getting ready

First we need to install the `RgoogleMaps` package and a related package `rgdal`:

```
install.packages("rgdal")
library(rgdal)

install.packages("RgoogleMaps")
library(RgoogleMaps)
```

We will use the `londonair.csv` example dataset for this recipe. This dataset contains annual average concentrations of particulate matter in London's atmosphere measured at 12 different air quality monitoring sites across the city (data source: London air website http://www.londonair.org.uk). So let's load that too:

```
air<-read.csv("londonair.csv")
```

How to do it...

Let's pull a Google map of London city and plot the pollution data as points on top of it:

```
london<-GetMap(center=c(51.51,-0.116),
zoom =10, destfile = "London.png",maptype = "mobile")

PlotOnStaticMap(london,lat = air$lat, lon = air$lon,
cex=2,pch=19,col=as.character(air$color))
```

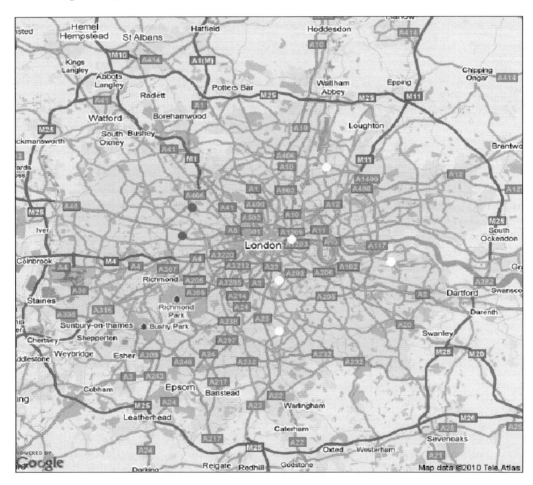

Now let's make the same graph with a satellite image map instead of the roadmap:

```
london<-GetMap(center=c(51.51,-0.116),zoom =13,
destfile = "London_satellite.png",maptype = "satellite")
```

```
PlotOnStaticMap(london,lat = air$lat, lon = air$lon,
cex=2,pch=19,col=as.character(air$color))
```

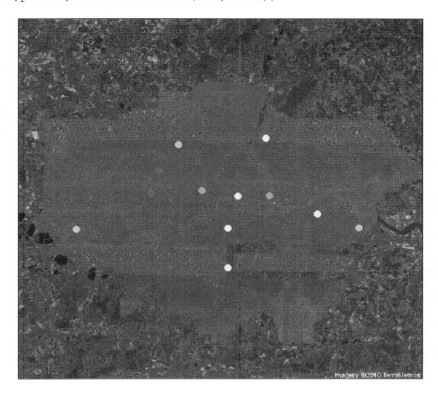

How it works...

In the examples, we first used the `GetMap()` function from the `RgoogleMaps` package to pull a map of London from the Google Static Maps API (see `http://code.google.com/apis/maps/documentation/staticmaps/` for more details about the API). We then used the `PlotOnStaticMap()` function to overlay our air pollution data points on the map.

The first and most important argument to the `GetMap()` function is the `center` argument, which takes a vector of two values specifying the latitude and longitude of the location to be used as the center of the map. The zoom level is specified by the `zoom` argument, which has a default value of 12. The higher the value of zoom, the more detailed and zoomed in the view. In the example, we set zoom to 10 so as to capture a wide area of London.

We also specified the `destfile` argument to save the retrieved map as `London.png`. The default value of `destfile` is `MyTile.png`. You can check whether the map is retrieved by looking for the PNG file in your working folder.

Finally, we also set the `maptype` argument, which can take one of a number of different values such as `"roadmap"`, `"mobile"`, `"satellite"`, `"terrain"`, `"hybrid"`, `"mapmaker-roadmap"`, and `"mapmaker-hybrid"`. The default map type is `terrain`. We set `maptype` to `mobile` in the first example and `satellite` in the second example.

If you look at the output of the `GetMap()` function call at the R prompt you will notice that it shows a URL such as:

```
[1] http://maps.google.com/staticmap?center=51.51,-0.116&zoom=10&size=
640x640&maptype=mobile&format=png32&key=&sensor=true
```

Basically, the `GetMap()` function creates an HTTP GET request URL with parameters based on the arguments supplied. To test this, copy the provided URL and paste it into the address bar of a web browser. You should get the image of the specified map.

We saved the object returned by the `GetMap()` function call as `london`, which we then passed as the first argument to the `PlotOnStaticMap()` function. As the name suggests, this function plots data on top of `map` objects. The air pollution dataset `londonair.csv` that we loaded earlier contains monitoring site data including site code, name, latitude, longitude, particle concentration (PM10), and a color based on the concentration value. We passed these values to the `PlotOnStaticMap()` function. We set the `lat` and `lon` arguments to the `lat` and `lon` columns in the air data frame respectively. We set the `col` argument to the color column in air.

There's more...

We can overlay more data points or lines successively on top of a map by setting an additional argument `add` to `TRUE`. By default, `add` is set to `FALSE` which creates a new map with the specified data points or lines. To draw lines instead of points, we need to set the `FUN` (meaning function) argument to `lines`. By default, `FUN` is set to `points`.

The following is another example pulling in a hybrid map of New York:

```
GetMap(center=c(40.714728,-73.99867), zoom =14,
    destfile = "Manhattan.png", maptype = "hybrid");
```

Another maps library, which is becoming increasingly popular, is Open Street Map (`http://www.openstreetmap.org/`). It's a free and open source editable library, unlike Google's proprietary maps API. The following is an example based on the `GetMap.OSM()` function which uses the Open Street Map server:

```
GetMap.OSM(lonR= c(-74.67102, -74.63943),
    latR = c(40.33804,40.3556),scale = 7500,
    destfile = "PrincetonOSM.png")
```

`GetMap.OSM()` takes the ranges of longitude and latitude as two two-valued vectors `lonR` and `latR` respectively. The `scale` argument is analogous to the `zoom` argument for the Google API. The larger this value, the more detailed the resulting map.

In the next recipe we will learn how to interact with Google's KML language for expressing geographic data.

Creating and reading KML data

In this recipe, we will learn how to read and write geographic data in Google's Keyhole Markup Language (KML) format, which can be used to visualize geographic data with Google Earth and Google Maps.

Getting ready

We will use the rgdal package in this recipe. So let's make sure it's installed and load it:

```
install.packages("rgdal")
library(rgdal)
```

How to do it...

We will use data from the cities shapefile that's installed as part of the rgdal package. First we will write a KML file and then read it:

```
cities <- readOGR(system.file("vectors",
package = "rgdal")[1],"cities")

writeOGR(cities, "cities.kml", "cities", driver="KML")

df <- readOGR("cities.kml", "cities")
```

How it works...

In the preceding example, we first used the readOGR() function to read the cities shapefile dataset. The first argument is the folder (directory) where the data shapefile is and the second argument is the name of the shapefile (without the .shp extension). We stored the object returned by the readOGR() function as cities, which is of class SpatialPointsDataFrame.

To create a KML file, we used the writeOGR() function. We passed the cities object as the first argument. The second argument specifies the name of the output KML file, the third argument specifies the shapefile layer name (without extension), and the fourth argument is the driver (in this case KML).

To read the KML file back into R, we used the `readOGR()` function with only two arguments. The first argument specifies the KML data file to be read and the second argument specifies the name of the layer.

See also

In the next recipe, we will learn how to work with ESRI shapefiles.

Working with ESRI shapefiles

In this recipe we will learn how to read and write geographic data in the form of shapefiles (`.shp`), using Geographical Information Systems (GIS) software created by ESRI and some other similar software.

Getting ready

We are going to use the `maptools` package for this recipe. So let's install and load it first:

```
install.packages("maptools")
library(maptools)
```

How to do it...

We are going to read an example shapefile provided with the `maptools` package and plot it:

```
sfdata <- readShapeSpatial(system.file("shapes/sids.shp",
package="maptools")[1], proj4string=CRS("+proj=longlat"))

plot(sfdata, col="orange", border="white", axes=TRUE)
```

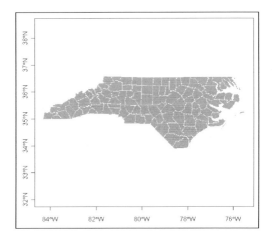

To write out the data as another shapefile we can do:

```
writeSpatialShape(sfdata, "xxpoly")
```

How it works...

We used the `readShapeSpatial()` function of the `maptools` package to read in a shapefile. This function takes a shapefile name as an argument and reads the data into a `SpatialPolygonsDataFrame` object. The first argument in the example is the path to the example shapefile `sids.shp` which is provided as part of the `maptools` package installation. The second argument `proj4string` specifies the projection type as `longlat` so that the spatial co-ordinates are interpreted correctly as longitudes and latitudes.

We saved the object returned by `readShapeSpatial()` as `sfdata` (of data class `SpatialPolygonsDataFrame`), which we then passed to the `plot()` function to create a map from the shapefile data.

Once we've read the data into the appropriate format, we can perform any transformations on the data. To save the transformed dataset back into a shapefile, we use the `writeSpatialShape()` function which takes the data object as the first argument and the name of the output shapefile (without any file type extension) as the second argument.

There's more...

There is another package called `shapefiles`, which can be used to read and write shapefiles. To use it, we must first install and load t:

```
install.packages("shapefiles")
library(shapefiles)
```

To read a shapefile using this package we can use the `read.shapefile()` function:

```
sf<-system.file("shapes/sids.shp", package="maptools")[1]
sf<-substr(sf,1,nchar(sf)-4)
sfdata <- read.shapefile(sf)
```

We first saved the path of the `sids.shp` example file in a variable called `sf`. We had to trim the path string to remove the extension `.shp` because the `read.shapefile()` function takes just the name of the shapefile as its argument. The shapefile data is saved in a list called `sfdata`.

To write out a shapefile using this package we need to use the `write.shapefile()` function:

```
write.shapefile(sfdata, "newsf")
```

The `write.shapefile()` takes two key arguments: the first is the data object (`sfdata` in the example) and the second is the name of the new shapefile without any file extension.

10
Finalizing graphs for publications and presentations

In this chapter, we will cover:

- ▶ Exporting graphs to high resolution image formats: PNG, JPEG, BMP, TIFF
- ▶ Exporting graphs to vector formats: SVG, PDF, PS
- ▶ Adding mathematical and scientific notations (typesetting)
- ▶ Adding text descriptions to graphs
- ▶ Using graph templates
- ▶ Choosing font families and styles under Windows, Mac OS X, and Linux
- ▶ Choosing fonts for PostScripts and PDFs

Introduction

In the previous chapters, we have learnt how to make graphs of different types and styles using various functions and arguments. In this chapter, we will learn some tricks and tips to add some polish to our graphs so that they can be used for publication and presentation.

We will look at the different image file formats we can save our graphs in and learn how to export our graphs at high resolutions. Most publications require authors to submit high resolution figures along with their manuscripts. We will also look in more detail at vector formats such as PDF, SVG, and PS, which are preferred by most publications since these are resolution-independent formats.

We will also learn how to add mathematical and scientific notations to graphs. These are indispensible in any scientific data visualization. We will also see how to add text descriptions inside graphs, which can be very handy as slides for presentation. Graph templates are a way to save time by creating functions which cut down repetitive code, so that once we are happy with the basic structure of a graph, we can experiment with various pre-defined themes to choose the most appropriate color combinations and styles.

Finally, we will also look at how to choose fonts under different operating systems and graphic devices. We will also learn how to add new font mappings and to choose additional font families for vector file formats.

As with the previous chapters, it is best to try out each recipe first with the example shown here and then with your own datasets so that you can fully understand each line of code. If you are preparing any graph for publication or presentation, it is also good practice to print out the saved graphs and verify that the printed output looks correct and clear.

Exporting graphs in high resolution image formats: PNG, JPEG, BMP, TIFF

In this recipe, we will learn how to save graphs in high resolution image formats for use in presentations and publications.

Getting ready

We are only using the base graphics functions for this recipe. So, just run the R code at the R prompt. You may wish to save the code as an R script so that you can use it again later.

How to do it...

Let's re-create a simple scatter plot example from *Chapter 1* and save it as PNG file 600 px high and 600 px wide with a resolution of 200 dots per inch (dpi):

```
png("cars.png",res=200,height=600,width=600)

plot(cars$dist~cars$speed,
main="Relationship between car distance and speed",
xlab="Speed (miles per hour)",ylab="Distance travelled (miles)",
xlim=c(0,30),ylim=c(0,140),
xaxs="i",yaxs="i",col="red",pch=19)

dev.off()
```

The resulting `cars.png` file looks like the following:

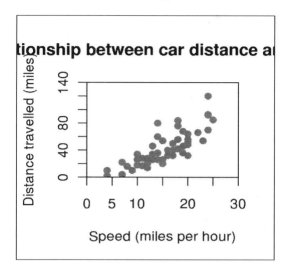

The pictured graph has a high resolution but the layout and formatting has been lost. So, let's create a high resolution PNG while preserving the formatting:

```
png("cars.png",res=200,height=600,width=600)

par(mar=c(4,4,3,1),omi=c(0.1,0.1,0.1,0.1),mgp=c(3,0.5,0),
las=1,mex=0.5,cex.main=0.6,cex.lab=0.5,cex.axis=0.5)

plot(cars$dist~cars$speed,
main="Relationship between car distance and speed",
xlab="Speed (miles per hour)",ylab="Distance travelled (miles)",
xlim=c(0,30),ylim=c(0,140),
xaxs="i",yaxs="i",
col="red",pch=19,cex=0.5)

dev.off()
```

The resulting PNG file looks like the following:

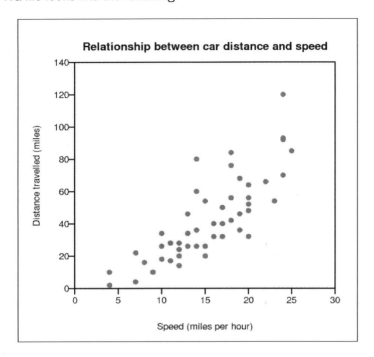

How it works...

To save our graph as a high resolution PNG (200 dpi), we had to set the `res` argument of the `png()` function to a value of `200`. The default value of `res` is `72`. We also set both the `height` and `width` arguments to `600`.

In the first example, we can see that simply specifying the resolution and dimensions of the PNG file is not enough. The resultant image loses its original formatting and layout. In addition to specifying the resolution and size, we also need to re-adjust the margins and sizes of various graph elements, including the data points, axis, plot titles, and axis labels. We set these parameters using the `par()` function and its arguments as we learnt in *Chapter 1* and *Chapter 2*.

To save the graphs as even higher resolution images, we would again need to adjust the relative margins and sizes of the graph components.

There's more...

To save a graph in other formats such as JPEG, BMP, and TIFF, we can use the `res` argument in the `jpeg()`, `bmp()`, and `tiff()` functions respectively.

In the next recipe, we will learn how to save graphs in vector formats.

Exporting graphs in vector formats: SVG, PDF, PS

In this recipe, we will learn how to save graphs in vector formats such as PDF, SVG, and PostScript (PS), which are resolution-independent.

Getting ready

Once again we will use the basic graph functions. So, just make sure you have started R and type the code at the R prompt.

How to do it...

Let's use the same scatter plot example from the previous recipe and save it in different vector formats, starting with PDF:

```
pdf("cars.pdf")

plot(cars$dist~cars$speed,
main="Relationship between car distance and speed",
xlab="Speed (miles per hour)",ylab="Distance travelled (miles)",
xlim=c(0,30),ylim=c(0,140),
xaxs="i",yaxs="i",
col="red",pch=19,cex=0.5)

dev.off()
```

Similarly, we can save the graph as SVG or PS using the `svg()` and `postscript()` functions respectively:

```
svg("3067_10_03.svg")
#plot command here
dev.off()

postscript("3067_10_03.ps")
#plot command here
dev.off()
```

How it works...

The vector format export commands are similar to the image format commands we saw in the previous recipe. First we open a new device by calling the `pdf()`, `svg()`, or `postscript()` functions with the output filename as its only argument, then issue the plot command and finally close the device with `dev.off()`.

> Windows users will have to use the `CairoSVG()` command in order to export files to SVG format. First import the `Cairo` package:
>
> ```
> install.packages("Cairo")
> library(Cairo)
> ```
>
> And then use the following commands:
>
> ```
> CairoSVG("3067_10_03.svg")
> #plot command here
> dev.off()
> ```

Since vector formats are resolution-independent, you can zoom in or out of them without losing any clarity of the graph. Size does not affect the resolution. So, unlike the image formats in the previous recipe, we did not have to re-adjust the graph margins and component sizes to save the graph as PDF, SVG, or PS.

There's more...

We can save more than one graph in a single PDF file by setting the `onefile` argument to `TRUE` (the default value). This is a useful output for presentations. All we have to do is issue the `pdf()` command with the output file name, then issue all the plot commands in the desired order and close the device with `dev.off()`. For example, let's make three variations of the cars plot with three different colors for the data points and save them into one file:

```
pdf("multiple.pdf")

for(i in 1:3)
  plot(cars,pch=19,col=i)

dev.off()
```

Another important setting when saving graphs in vector formats is the color model. Most publications require authors to use the CMYK (Cyan Magenta Yellow Key) color model in their graphs, instead of the default RGB (Red Green Blue) model. We can save our graphs as PDFs or PostScripts with the CMYK color model simply by setting the `colormodel` argument to `cmyk`:

```
pdf("multiple.pdf",colormodel="cmyk")

for(i in 1:3)
  plot(cars,pch=19,col=i)

dev.off()
```

By default, `colormodel` is set to `rgb`. The other possible value is `gray` for grayscale.

Adding mathematical and scientific notations (typesetting)

Producing graphs for scientific journals is rarely ever done without adding some special scientific and mathematical notations, such as subscripts, superscripts, symbols, and other notations. In this recipe we will learn how to add these to annotations to our graphs.

Getting ready

We are only using base graphics functions for this recipe. So, just open up the R prompt and type the following code. We will use the `airpollution.csv` example dataset for this recipe. So let's first load it:

```
air<-read.csv("airpollution.csv")
```

How to do it...

Let's make a scatter plot of concentrations of Particulate Matter(PM) versus Nitrogen Oxides(NO_x) and add titles with subscripts as in PM_{10} and NO_x and units mg m^{-3}:

```
plot(air,las=1,
main=expression(paste("Relationship between ",PM[10]," and ",NO[X])),
xlab=expression(paste(NO[X]," concentrations (",mu*g^-3,")")),
ylab=expression(paste(PM[10]," concentrations (",mu*g^-3,")")))
```

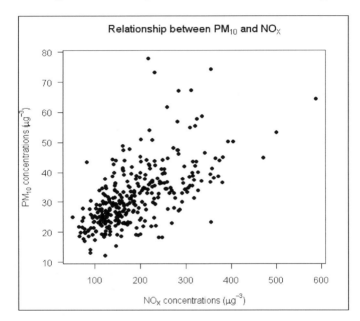

How it works...

In the example, we added three new elements of special formatting and notation: subscripts, superscripts, and a Greek symbol, using the `expression()` function.

The `expression()` function accepts arguments in a pre-defined syntax and translates them into the desired format or symbol. For example, any characters enclosed within square brackets `[]` are converted to subscripts, such as the X in NO_x and 10 in PM_{10}. Similarly, any characters following the `^` sign are converted to superscripts, such as the power value -3 in mg m^{-3}. The letters `mu` are converted to symbol μ denoting micro.

In the example, we used a combination of regular text and expressions by using the `expression()` function with the `paste()` function.

There's more...

There are a lot more options and functions we can use inside `expression()` to create a lot more advanced notations than subscripts and superscripts. For example, `integral()`, `frac()`, `sqrt()`, and `sum()` can be used to create mathematical signs for integrals, fractions, square roots, and sums respectively.

To see and learn all the possible options and symbols, run the following command at the R prompt:

```
demo(plotmath)
```

You will see the following symbols displayed on the plot device. You will need to press *Return* or *Enter* to progress through each set of symbols:

Arithmetic Operators		Radicals	
x + y	$x+y$	sqrt(x)	$\sqrt{x}$
x - y	$x-y$	sqrt(x, y)	$\sqrt[y]{x}$
x * y	xy	**Relations**	
x/y	x/y	x == y	$x = y$
x %+-% y	$x \pm y$	x != y	$x \neq y$
x%/%y	$x \div y$	x < y	$x < y$
x %*% y	$x \times y$	x <= y	$x \leq y$
x %.% y	$x \cdot y$	x > y	$x > y$
-x	$-x$	x >= y	$x \geq y$
+x	$+x$	x %~~% y	$x \approx y$
Sub/Superscripts		x %=~% y	$x \cong y$
x[i]	x_i	x %==% y	$x \equiv y$
x^2	x^2	x %prop% y	$x \propto y$
Juxtaposition		**Typeface**	
x * y	xy	plain(x)	x
paste(x, y, z)	xyz	italic(x)	x
Lists		bold(x)	$\mathbf{x}$
list(x, y, z)	x, y, z	bolditalic(x)	$\boldsymbol{x}$
		underline(x)	$\underline{x}$

Ellipsis		Arrows	
list(x[1], ..., x[n])	$x_1, \ldots, x_n$	x %<->% y	$x \leftrightarrow y$
x[1] + ... + x[n]	$x_1 + \cdots + x_n$	x %->% y	$x \rightarrow y$
list(x[1], cdots, x[n])	$x_1, \cdots, x_n$	x %<-% y	$x \leftarrow y$
x[1] + ldots + x[n]	$x_1 + \ldots + x_n$	x %up% y	$x \uparrow y$
Set Relations		x %down% y	$x \downarrow y$
x %subset% y	$x \subset y$	x %<=>% y	$x \Leftrightarrow y$
x %subseteq% y	$x \subseteq y$	x %=>% y	$x \Rightarrow y$
x %supset% y	$x \supset y$	x %<=% y	$x \Leftarrow y$
x %supseteq% y	$x \supseteq y$	x %dblup% y	$x \Uparrow y$
x %notsubset% y	$x \not\subset y$	x %dbldown% y	$x \Downarrow y$
x %in% y	$x \in y$	**Symbolic Names**	
x %notin% y	$x \notin y$	Alpha - Omega	$A - \Omega$
Accents		alpha - omega	$\alpha - \omega$
hat(x)	$\hat{x}$	phi1 + sigma1	$\varphi + \varsigma$
tilde(x)	$\tilde{x}$	Upsilon1	Υ
ring(x)	$\mathring{x}$	infinity	∞
bar(xy)	$\overline{xy}$	32 * degree	$32°$
widehat(xy)	$\widehat{xy}$	60 * minute	$60'$
widetilde(xy)	$\widetilde{xy}$	30 * second	$30''$

Style	
displaystyle(x)	x
textstyle(x)	x
scriptstyle(x)	x
scriptscriptstyle(x)	x
Spacing	
x ~ ~y	$x \; y$

x + phantom(0) + y	$x + \quad + y$
x + over(1, phantom(0))	$x + \dfrac{1}{}$
Fractions	
frac(x, y)	$\dfrac{x}{y}$
over(x, y)	$\dfrac{x}{y}$
atop(x, y)	$\genfrac{}{}{0pt}{}{x}{y}$

Big Operators	
sum(x[i], i = 1, n)	$\sum\limits_{1}^{n} x_i$
prod(plain(P)(X == x), x)	$\prod\limits_{x} P(X = x)$
integral(f(x) * dx, a, b)	$\int\limits_{a}^{b} f(x)dx$
union(A[i], i == 1, n)	$\bigcup\limits_{i=1}^{n} A_i$
intersect(A[i], i == 1, n)	$\bigcap\limits_{i=1}^{n} A_i$
lim(f(x), x %->% 0)	$\lim\limits_{x \to 0} f(x)$
min(g(x), x >= 0)	$\min\limits_{x \geq 0} g(x)$
inf(S)	$\inf S$
sup(S)	$\sup S$

Grouping	
(x + y) * z	$(x+y)z$
x^y + z	$x^y + z$
x^(y + z)	$x^{(y+z)}$
x^{y + z}	x^{y+z}
group("(", list(a, b), "]")	$(a, b]$
bgroup("(", atop(x, y), ")")	$\binom{x}{y}$
group(lceil, x, rceil)	$\lceil x \rceil$
group(lfloor, x, rfloor)	$\lfloor x \rfloor$
group("|", x, "|")	$\|x\|$

Adding text descriptions to graphs

Sometimes we may wish to add descriptions to a graph, say if we are producing a PDF for presentation or as a handout with notes. In this recipe, we will learn how to add text descriptions in the margins of a graph, instead of having to add it separately in another program.

Getting ready

We are only using the base graphics functions for this recipe. So, just open up the R prompt and type the code we are about to see. You may wish to save the code as an R script for later use.

How to do it...

Let's plot a random normal distribution and add a little bit of description below the graph:

```
par(mar=c(12,4,3,2))
plot(rnorm(1000),main="Random Normal Distribution")

desc<-expression(paste("The normal distribution has density ",
f(x) == frac(1,sqrt(2*pi)*sigma)~ plain(e)^frac(-(x-mu)^2,2*sigma^2)))

mtext(desc,side=1,line=4,padj=1,adj=0)

mtext(expression(paste("where ", mu, " is the mean of the distribution
and ",sigma," the standard deviation.")),
side=1,line=7,padj=1,adj=0)
```

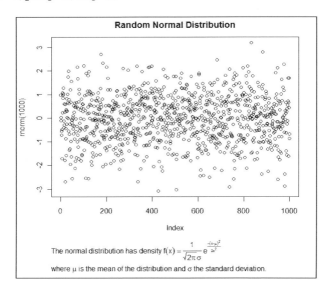

How it works...

In the example, we set the bottom margin of the plot to a high value and used the `mtext()` function to add a small description below the graph.

We created an expression called `desc` with the `expression()` function we saw in the previous recipe and used `mtext()` to place it in the fourth line of the bottom margin. To make the text top-left aligned we set `padj` to `1` and `adj` to `0`. We used `mtext()` again to place the other half of the description on the seventh line of the margin. We had to split the description into two halves and use `mtext()` twice because we couldn't automatically line wrap an expression. We will soon see another example with a text-only description, where we can wrap it in just one `mtext()` function call.

There's more...

Let's look at another example, where we add the description above the graph but just below the title. This time the description will just be plain text and will not contain any expressions. We will use the `dailysales.csv` example dataset and make a line graph of daily sales data:

```
dailysales<-read.csv("dailysales.csv")

par(mar=c(5,5,12,2))

plot(units~as.Date(date,"%d/%m/%y"),data=dailysales,type="l",
las=1,ylab="Units Sold",xlab="Date")

desc<-"The graph below shows sales data for Product A in the month of
January 2010. There were a lot of ups and downs in the number of units
sold. The average number of units sold was around 5000. The highest
sales were recorded on the 27th January, nearly 7000 units sold."

mtext(paste(strwrap(desc,width=80),collapse="\
n"),side=3,line=3,padj=0,adj=0)

title("Daily Sales Trends",line=10,adj=0,font=2)
```

This will produce the following graph:

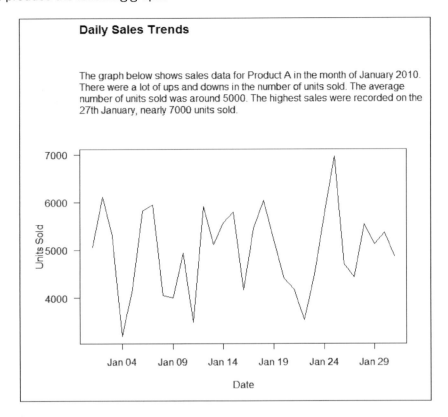

In the example, we set the margins such that the top margin is 12 lines wide. We created a string called desc with the description for the graph. We then used mtext() to place the string in the third line of the margin. We couldn't simply pass desc to mtext() because it wouldn't fit within the width of the plot area and would get chopped off after the first sentence. So we used the strwrap() function to wrap the string with a width of 80 characters. We used the paste() function to join the split strings created by strwrap(), with line breaks added by setting the collapse argument to "\n". Finally, we used the title() function to add a graph title on top.

Using graph templates

We may often find ourselves using similar code repetitively to plot similar kinds of data or different versions of the same dataset. Once we have analyzed our data and are looking to produce a finished graph, it can be useful to quickly try out different color combinations and other aesthetic settings without having to write too much repetitive code. In this recipe, we will learn how to create graph templates and use them to quickly try out various "looks" for a graph.

Getting ready

We are only using the base graphics functions for this recipe. So, just open up the R prompt and type the following code. We will use the `themes.csv` file which contains theme parameters for this recipe. So let's first load it:

```
themes<-read.csv("themes.csv")
```

How to do it...

We will make a simple scatter plot showing a random normal distribution, and apply different color combination themes to it with a single command:

```
themeplot<-function(x,theme,...) {
    i<-which(themes$theme==theme)
    par(bg=as.character(themes[i,]$bg_color),las=1)

    plot(x,type="n",...)

    u<-par("usr")
    plotcol=as.character(themes[i,]$plot_color)
    rect(u[1],u[3],u[2],u[4],col=plotcol,border=plotcol)

    points(x,col=as.character(themes[i,]$symbol_color),...)
    box()
}
```

Using this function, we can create a scatter plot using different themes such as the following:

```
themeplot(rnorm(1000),theme="white",pch=21,main="White")
```

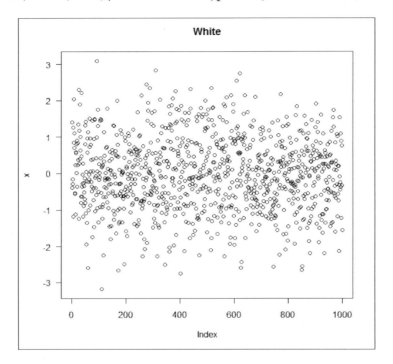

```
themeplot(rnorm(1000),theme="lightgray",pch=21,main="Light Gray")
```

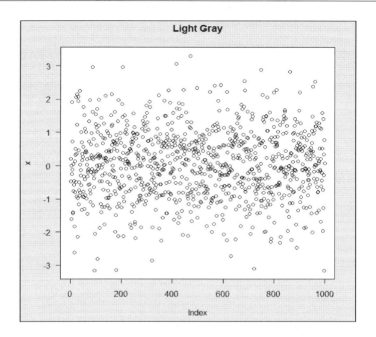

```
themeplot(rnorm(1000),theme="dark",pch=21,main="Dark")
```

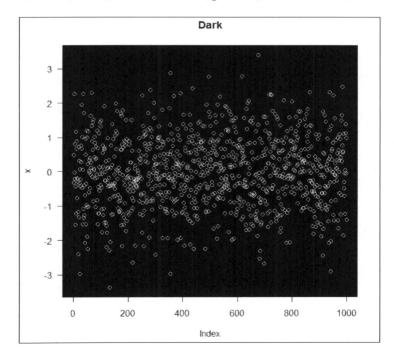

```
themeplot(rnorm(1000),theme="pink",pch=21,main="Pink")
```

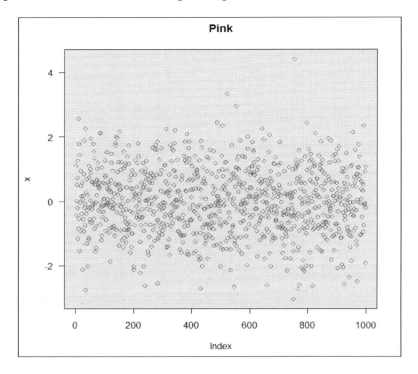

How it works...

In the preceding example, we created a function called themeplot(), which used pre-defined color combinations from the themes.csv file to create different themed graphs.

We first read the themes.csv file into a data frame called themes, which contains four columns:

- ▶ theme (name of the theme)
- ▶ bg_color (figure background color)
- ▶ plot_color (plot region color)
- ▶ symbol_color (color of plotting symbol)

We then created the themeplot() function which accepts the plotting variable x and theme as arguments. The trailing " . . . " means that additional arguments can be passed which are passed on to the specified functions within the themeplot() function definition. themeplot() uses the which() function to find the row index of the specified theme and then uses the corresponding column values to set the figure background color in par(), the plot region color in rect(), and symbol color in points().

Once the function is defined, all we have to do to try out different color combinations is pass the `theme` argument to `themeplot()`. If we wish to modify the color combinations or add new themes we can simply edit the `themes.csv` file and re-read it. We can also adjust the function definition so that we can pass the color values separately to override the theme specifications.

There's more...

In the example, we chose some very simple color parameters to demonstrate the usefulness of themes. However, we could easily add more columns to the themes definitions, such as symbol types, sizes, line types and colors, fonts, grid line styles, legend styles, and so on. It is best to work with your own dataset and define themes as you go along and have a better idea of what your specific requirements are. Once you have the structure of the graph decided, you can define various themes to quickly experiment and choose from.

Choosing font families and styles under Windows, Mac OS X, and Linux

In this recipe we will see how to choose font families and styles under the three most popular operating systems, namely, Windows, Mac OS X, and Linux.

Getting ready

We are only using base graphics functions for this recipe. So, just open up the R prompt and type the following code. You may wish to save the code as an R script for later use.

How to do it...

Let's look at all the basic default fonts available under Windows:

```
par(mar=c(1,1,5,1))
plot(1:200,type="n",main="Fonts under Windows",axes=FALSE,xlab="",
ylab="")

text(0,180,"Arial \n(family=\"sans\", font=1)",
family="sans",font=1,adj=0)
text(0,140,"Arial Bold \n(family=\"sans\", font=2)",
family="sans",font=2,adj=0)
text(0,100,"Arial Italic \n(family=\"sans\", font=3)",
family="sans",font=3,adj=0)
text(0,60,"Arial Bold Italic \n(family=\"sans\", font=4)",
family="sans",font=4,adj=0)

text(70,180,"Times \n(family=\"serif\", font=1)",
```

```
family="serif",font=1,adj=0)
text(70,140,"Times Bold \n(family=\"serif\", font=2)",
family="serif",font=2,adj=0)
text(70,100,"Times Italic \n(family=\"serif\", font=3)",
family="serif",font=3,adj=0)
text(70,60,"Times Bold Italic \n(family=\"serif\", font=4)",
family="serif",font=4,adj=0)

text(130,180,"Courier New\n(family=\"mono\", font=1)",
family="mono",font=1,adj=0)
text(130,140,"Courier New Bold \n(family=\"mono\", font=2)",
family="mono",font=2,adj=0)
text(130,100,"Courier New Italic \n(family=\"mono\", font=3)",
family="mono",font=3,adj=0)
text(130,60,"Courier New Bold Italic \n(family=\"mono\",
font=4)",
family="mono",font=4,adj=0)
```

Fonts under Windows

Arial
(family="sans", font=1)

Times
(family="serif", font=1)

Courier New
(family="mono", font=1)

Arial Bold
(family="sans", font=2)

Times Bold
(family="serif", font=2)

Courier New Bold
(family="mono", font=2)

Arial Italic
(family="sans", font=3)

Times Italic
(family="serif", font=3)

Courier New Italic
(family="mono", font=3)

Arial Bold Italic
(family="sans", font=4)

Times Bold Italic
(family="serif", font=4)

Courier New Bold Italic
(family="mono", font=4)

How it works...

In the example, we demonstrated all the combinations of the basic font faces and families available in R under Windows. Fonts are specified in R by choosing a font family and a font face. There are three main font families: sans, serif, and mono, which are mapped on to specific fonts under different operating systems. As shown in the example, under Windows sans maps to Arial, serif to Times New Roman and mono to Courier New. The font family is specified by the family argument, which can be passed to the text() function (as in the example) or in par() (thus applied to all text in the plot), mtext(), and title().

The font face can take four basic values denoted by the numbers `1` to `4`, which stand for regular, bold, italic, and bold italic respectively. The default value of font is `1`. Note that font only applies to text inside the plot area. To set the font face for axis annotations, labels and the plot title, we need to use `font.axis`, `font.lab`, and `font.main` respectively.

In the example, we created a plot area with X and Y co-ordinates running from `0` to `200` each, but suppressed drawing of any axes or annotations. Then we used the `text()` function to draw text labels showing the 12 combinations of the three font families and four font faces.

There's more...

As you may have noticed, we did not specify the names of the font families in the `text()` command. Instead we used the keywords `sans`, `serif`, and `mono` to refer to the corresponding default fonts under Windows. We can check these font family mappings by running the `windowsFonts()` command at the R prompt, which lists the names of the fonts for each of the font families. We can also add new mappings using this function. For example, to add the font Georgia we need to run:

```
windowsFonts(GE = windowsFont("Georgia"))
```

Then we can just set family to `"GE"` to use the Georgia font:

```
text(150,80,"Georgia",family="GE")
```

Just like under Windows, there are default font families under Mac OS X and Linux. The serif and mono fonts are the same as in Windows. However the sans font is usually Helvetica. To check the default font mappings and add new font families, we need to use the `X11Fonts()` and `quartzFonts()` functions under Linux and OS X respectively.

See also

In the next recipe we will see how to use additional font families available for vector formats such as PDF and PS.

Choosing fonts for PostScripts and PDFs

The `pdf` and `postscript` graphic devices in R have special functions that handle the translation of an R graphics font family name to a PostScript or PDF file. In this recipe, we will see how to choose the fonts for these vector formats.

Getting ready

We are only using the base graphics functions for this recipe. So, just open up the R prompt and type the code we are about to see. You may wish to save the code as an R script for later use.

How to do it...

Let's create a PDF of an `rnorm()` graph with the title and axis annotations in the font Avant Garde:

```
pdf("fonts.pdf",family="AvantGarde")
plot(rnorm(100),main="Random Normal Distribution")
dev.off()
```

To save the same graph as a PostScript file, we can do:

```
postscript("fonts.ps",family="AvantGarde")
plot(rnorm(100),main="Random Normal Distribution")
dev.off()
```

How it works...

As shown in the examples, the font family for a PDF or PostScript output is set exactly the same way as in the previous recipe, by using the `family` argument. In the examples, we passed the `family` argument to the `pdf()` and `postscript()` functions since they open the relevant graphics devices.

Note that we used a font family which was not available in the basic R graphics device. We can also use the default values `sans`, `serif`, and `mono`, which are mapped to Helvetica, Times New Roman, and Courier New respectively. The `pdf` and `postscript` devices have inbuilt mappings to a lot of font families. To see all the available fonts, we can use the `pdfFonts()` command. Running `pdfFonts()` at the R prompt lists all the names of the font families and related attributes (metrics, encoding, and class). To list just the names of all font families we can run:

```
names(pdfFonts())
```

That gives the following output at the R prompt:

```
 [1] "serif"            "sans"               "mono"
 [4] "AvantGarde"       "Bookman"            "Courier"
 [7] "Helvetica"        "Helvetica-Narrow"   "NewCenturySchoolbook"
[10] "Palatino"         "Times"              "URWGothic"
[13] "URWBookman"       "NimbusMon"          "NimbusSan"
[16] "URWHelvetica"     "NimbusSanCond"      "CenturySch"
[19] "URWPalladio"      "NimbusRom"          "URWTimes"
[22] "Japan1"           "Japan1HeiMin"       "Japan1GothicBBB"
[25] "Japan1Ryumin"     "Korea1"             "Korea1deb"
[28] "CNS1"             "GB1"
```

We can check the default mapping to sans by running `pdfFonts()$sans` at the R prompt.

There's more...

The `postscript` device has two extra fonts: Computer Modern and Computer Modern Italic (you can check this by running `names(postscriptFonts())` at the R prompt). Just like the commands for specific operating systems, we can use `pdfFonts()` and `postscriptFonts()` to add new font mappings for the `pdf` and `postscript` devices respectively. Please refer to the help section to see some examples of such mappings (`?postscriptFonts()` and `?pdfFonts()`).

Index

H

heat.colors() function
about 46, 187
example 46, 47
heat.colors() palette 53
heatmap() function
about 26, 184
using 25
heat maps
about 24, 26, 181
calendar heat maps 199
correlation heat maps 185
creating 25, 26
example 26, 27
with single Z variable along X and Y axes 182
heat maps, of single Z variable with scale
creating 182-184
height argument 226
heights argument 157
high resolution image formats
graphs, saving into 224-226
hist() function
about 46
using 146, 147
histograms
about 146
creating 18-20
drawing, in margins of bivariate scatter plot 155-157
embedding, in another kind of graph 153-155
kernel density lines, imposing on 152, 153
histogram styles
adjusting 150, 151
Hmisc package 82
horiz argument 15, 98, 129, 130
horizontal argument 168
horizontal bars
orientation, adjusting 128, 129
horizontal boxes
box plots, creating with 167, 168
horizontal error bars
drawing 80
horizontal grid lines
adding, to graphs 102

human readable time formats
axis labels, annotating in 113, 114

I

image file format
graphs, saving as 40, 41
image() function
about 184, 188, 209
correlation heat map, creating 26, 27
installation, RgoogleMaps package 215
integral() function 231

J

jitter() function
about 82, 84
closely packed data points, distinguishing 82-84

K

Keyhole Markup Language *See* **KML data**
KML data
creating 219
reading 219

L

labels
placing, inside bars 134, 135
labels argument 139
las argument
about 161
using 64
lattice library 214
lattice package 70
layout() function
about 184, 209
arguments 157
using 156
legend() function
about 35, 125, 128, 143
arguments 97, 98
using 97

width
   selecting 58-60
width argument 131, 162, 226
widths argument 157
Windows
   fonts, selecting under 241, 242
windowsFonts() command 243
write.shapefile() function 221

X

X axes limits
   adjusting, for plots 22-24
X axis
   formatted date values, plotting on 112
   formatted time values, plotting on 112

   marker lines, adding at 104, 105
xaxp argument 63, 64
xyplot() command 70-72

Y

Y axes limits
   adjusting, for plots 22-24
Y axis
   marker lines, adding at 104, 105
yaxp argument 63, 64

Z

zoo() function 111

Thank you for buying
R Graphs Cookbook

About Packt Publishing

Packt, pronounced 'packed', published its first book "*Mastering phpMyAdmin for Effective MySQL Management*" in April 2004 and subsequently continued to specialize in publishing highly focused books on specific technologies and solutions.

Our books and publications share the experiences of your fellow IT professionals in adapting and customizing today's systems, applications, and frameworks. Our solution based books give you the knowledge and power to customize the software and technologies you're using to get the job done. Packt books are more specific and less general than the IT books you have seen in the past. Our unique business model allows us to bring you more focused information, giving you more of what you need to know, and less of what you don't.

Packt is a modern, yet unique publishing company, which focuses on producing quality, cutting-edge books for communities of developers, administrators, and newbies alike. For more information, please visit our website: www.packtpub.com.

About Packt Open Source

In 2010, Packt launched two new brands, Packt Open Source and Packt Enterprise, in order to continue its focus on specialization. This book is part of the Packt Open Source brand, home to books published on software built around Open Source licences, and offering information to anybody from advanced developers to budding web designers. The Open Source brand also runs Packt's Open Source Royalty Scheme, by which Packt gives a royalty to each Open Source project about whose software a book is sold.

Writing for Packt

We welcome all inquiries from people who are interested in authoring. Book proposals should be sent to author@packtpub.com. If your book idea is still at an early stage and you would like to discuss it first before writing a formal book proposal, contact us; one of our commissioning editors will get in touch with you.

We're not just looking for published authors; if you have strong technical skills but no writing experience, our experienced editors can help you develop a writing career, or simply get some additional reward for your expertise.

open source *
community experience distilled
.SHING

Statistical Analysis with R

ISBN: 978-1-849512-08-4   Paperback: 376 pages

Take control of your data and produce superior statistical analysis with R.

1. An easy introduction for people who are new to R, with plenty of strong examples for you to work through

2. This book will take you on a journey to learn R as the strategist for an ancient Chinese kingdom!

3. A step by step guide to understand R, its benefits, and how to use it to maximize the impact of your data analysis

4. A practical guide to conduct and communicate your data analysis with R in the most effective manner

OpenStreetMap

ISBN: 978-1-847197-50-4   Paperback: 252 pages

Be your own cartographer

1. Collect data for the area you want to map with this OpenStreetMap book and eBook

2. Create your own custom maps to print or use online following our proven tutorials

3. Collaborate with other OpenStreetMap contributors to improve the map data

4. Learn how OpenStreetMap works and why it's different to other sources of geographical information with this professional guide

Please check **www.PacktPub.com** for information on our titles

Python Geospatial Development

ISBN: 978-1-849511-54-4   Paperback: 508 pages

Build a complete and sophisticated mapping application from scratch using Python tools for GIS development

1. Build applications for GIS development using Python

2. Analyze and visualize Geo-Spatial data

3. Comprehensive coverage of key GIS concepts

4. Recommended best practices for storing spatial data in a database

5. Draw maps, place data points onto a map, and interact with maps

Plone 3 for Education

ISBN: 978-1-847198-12-9   Paperback: 193 pages

Break the webmaster bottleneck by empowering instructors and staff

1. Enable instructors and staff to represent courses using Plone's built-in content types—news items, collections, and events—without writing a single line of code

2. Embed sound and video into your course materials, news feeds, or anywhere on your Plone site

3. Written by Erik Rose—member of the Plone 4 and 5 Framework Teams

4. Expert guidance on using the best plug-ins so that you can get the best out of your site right from the beginning

Please check **www.PacktPub.com** for information on our titles

2429668R00145

Printed in Great Britain
by Amazon.co.uk, Ltd.,
Marston Gate.